WAKE UP
AND LIVE!

By Dorothea Brande

SIMON AND SCHUSTER

NEW YORK · 1936

1st Printing	5000 copies
2nd Printing	3000 copies
3rd Printing	5000 copies
4th Printing	5000 copies
5th Printing	5000 copies
6th Printing	10000 copies
7th Printing	12000 copies
8th Printing	5000 copies
9th Printing	15000 copies
10th Printing	10000 copies
11th Printing	25000 copies
12th Printing	10000 copies
13th Printing	15000 copies
Total	125000 copies

CONTENTS

INTRODUCTION

Two years ago I came across a formula for success which has revolutionized my life. It was so simple, and so obvious once I had seen it, that I could hardly believe it was responsible for the magical results which followed my putting it into practice.

The first thing to confess is that two years ago I was a failure. Oh, nobody knew it except me and those who knew me well enough to see that I was not doing a tenth of what could be expected of me. I held an interesting position, lived not too dull a life—yet there was no doubt in my own mind, at least, that I had failed. What I was doing was a substitute activity for what I had planned to do; and no matter how ingenious and neat the theories were which I presented to myself to account for my lack of success, I knew very well that there was more work that I should be doing, and better work, and work more demonstrably my own.

Of course I was always looking for a way out of my impasse. But when I actually had the good fortune to find it, I hardly believed in my own luck. At first I did not try to analyze or explain it. For one thing, the effects of using the formula were so remarkable that I was almost on the verge of being superstitious about the matter; it seemed like magic, and it doesn't do to inquire too closely into the reasons for a spell or incantation! More realistic than that, there was—at that time—still a trace of wariness about my attitude. I had tried to get out of my difficulties many times before, had often seemed to be about to do so, and then had found them closing in around me again as relentlessly as ever. But the main reason for my taking so little time to analyze or explain the effects of the formula after I once began to use it consistently was that I was much too busy and having far too much fun. It was enough to revel in the ease with which I did work hitherto impossible for me, to see barriers I had thought impenetrable melt away, to feel the inertia and timidity which had bound me for years dropping off like unlocked fetters.

For I had been years in my deadlock; I had known what I wanted to do, had equipped myself for my profession—and got nowhere. Yet I had chosen my life-work, which was writing, early, and had started out with high hopes. Most of the work I had finished had met a friendly reception. But then when I tried to take the next step and go on to a more mature phase it was as though I had been turned to stone. I felt as if I could not *start.*

Of course it goes without saying that I was unhappy. Not miserably and painfully unhappy, but just nagged at and depressed by my own ineffectuality. I busied myself at editing, since I seemed doomed to fail at the more creative side of literature; and I never ceased harrying myself, consulting teachers and analysts and psychologists and physicians for advice as to how to get out of my pit. I read and inquired and thought and worried; I tried every suggestion for relief. Nothing worked more than temporarily. For a while I might engage in feverish activity, but never for more than a week or two. Then the period of action would suddenly end, leaving me as far from my goal as ever, and each time more deeply discouraged.

Then, between one minute and the next, I found the idea which set me free. This time I was not con-

sciously looking for it; I was engaged on a piece of research in quite another field. But I came across a sentence in the book I was reading, HUMAN PER-SONALITY, *by F. W. H. Myers, which was so illuminating that I put the book aside to consider all the ideas suggested in that one penetrating hypothesis. When I picked up the book again I was a different person.*

Every aspect, attitude, relation of my life was altered. At first, as I say, I did not realize that. I only knew, with increasing certainty from day to day, that at last I had found a talisman for counter-acting failure and inertia and discouragement and that it worked. That was quite enough for me! *My hands and my days were so full that there was no time for introspection. I did sometimes drop off to sleep, after doing in a short while what once would have seemed to me a gigantic task, thinking, like the old lady of the nursery rhyme, "This is none of I!" But "I" was reaping the rewards, beyond doubt: the books I had wanted to write for so long and had so agonizingly failed to write were flowing, now, as fast as the words would go on paper, and so far from feeling drained by the activity, I was continually finding new ideas which had been hidden, as it were, behind the work that had "backed up" in my mind and made a barrier.*

Here is the total amount of writing I was able to do in the twenty years before I found my formula—the little writing which I was painfully, laboriously, protestingly able to do. For safety's sake I have over-estimated the items in each classification, so a generous estimate of it comes to this: Seventeen short stories, twenty book-reviews, half a dozen newspaper items, one attempt at a novel, abandoned less than a third of the way through. An average of less than two completed pieces of work per year!

For the two years after my moment of illumination, this is the record: Three books (the first two in just two weeks less than the first year, and both successful in their different fields), twenty-four articles, four short stories, seventy-two lectures, the scaffolding of three more books; and innumerable letters of consultation and professional advice sent to all parts of the country.

Nor are those by any means the only results of applying my formula. As soon as I discovered how it worked in the one matter of releasing my energy for writing, I began to be curious as to what else it might do for me, and to try acting upon it in other fields where I had had trouble. The tentativeness and timidity which had crippled me in almost every aspect of my life dropped away. Interviews, lectures, engagements which I had driven myself to, going against the grain every minute, became pleasurable experiences. On the other hand, a dozen stupid little exploitations of myself which I had allowed—almost in a penitential spirit—so long as I was in my deadlock were ended then and there. I was on good terms with myself at last, no longer punishing and exhorting and ruthlessly driving myself, and so no longer allowing myself to be unnecessarily bored and tired.

Although my formula had worked with such striking consequences for me, I told very few of my friends about it. In the almost fatuous egotism which I seem to share with ninety-nine one-hundredths of my fellows, I thought my case was unique: that no one had ever got into quite such a state of ineffectiveness before, nor would be able to apply the formula I used so successfully on his own difficulties. From time to time, now that I was no longer living in such a state of siege as made me blind to all outside happenings,

I did see indications here and there that another was wasting his life in much the same way that I had wasted mine; but I had had the good fortune to emerge and so, I thought, would he, in good time. Except for chance I would never have thought of publicly offering the simple program which had helped me so; I might, indeed, never have realized that to a greater or less extent most adults are living inadequate lives and suffering in consequence.

But some months ago I was asked to lecture to a group of book-sellers, and the subject which was tentatively given me was "The Difficulties of Becoming a Writer". Now in my first book I had gone into those difficulties pretty thoroughly; I had no desire to read a chapter from an already published book to an audience the members of which were in a little better way to have read the chapter than almost any other group would have been. Beginning to prepare the lecture I could think of nothing further to add to the subject than to say frankly that the most difficult of all tasks for a writer was learning to counteract his own inertia and cowardice. So, fearing at first that my talk would have somewhat the sound of "testifying to grace" in an old-fashioned prayer-meeting, I began to consider the subject and prepare my speech.

The conclusions I came to are in this book: that we are victims to a Will to Fail; that unless we see this in time and take action against it we die without accomplishing our intentions; that there is a way of counteracting that Will which gives results that seem like magic. I gave my lecture. What was really startling to me was to see how it was received. Until the notes, the letters, the telephone-calls began to come in, I had thought the report of how one person overcame a dilemma might interest many of the audience mildly and help two or three hearers who found themselves in somewhat the same plight.

But it seemed that my audience, almost to a man, was in the state I had described, that they all were looking for help to get out of it. I gave the lecture twice more; the results were the same. I was flooded with messages, questions, and requests for interviews. Best of all were three reports which came to me within two weeks. Three of my hearers had not waited for a fuller exposition, or taken it for granted that the formula would not work for them, but had

—8—

put it into immediate practice. One had written and sold a story which had haunted her for years, but which had seemed too "extraordinary" to be likely to sell. A man had gone home and quietly ended the exploitation of himself by a temperamental sister, and had made arrangements to resume evening work in a line that he had abandoned at his sister's insistence; to his astonishment, his sister, once she thoroughly understood that he refused to be handicapped longer, had seemed to wake from a long period of peevish hypochondria and was happier than she had been in years. The third case was too long and too personal to recount here, but in many ways it was the best of them all. Well, there were three persons, at least, who found the formula efficacious; and, like me, each of them found something rather awe-inspiring about the results.

We all live so far below the possible level for our lives that when we are set free from the things which hamper us so that we merely approach the potentialities in ourselves, we seem to have been entirely transfigured. It is in comparison with the halting, tentative, hesitant lives we let ourselves live that the

*full, normal life that is ours by right seems to par-
take of the definitely supernormal. When that is seen,
it is easy to discover that all men and women of
effective lives, whether statesmen, philosophers, artists
or men of business, use, sometimes entirely unconsciously, the same mental attitude in which to do
their work that their less fortunate fellows must
either find for themselves or die without discovering.
Occasionally, as the reading of biographies and
autobiographies shows, enlightenment comes through
religion, philosophy, or whole-hearted admiration
for another; and the individual, although often feeling still weak in himself, is sustained by his devo-
tion, is often capable of feats of endurance, effectiveness or genius which cause us to marvel at him. But
those who are not born with this knowledge of the
way to induce the state in which successful work is
done, who do not learn it so early that they cannot
remember a time when they did not know it, or who
for some reason cannot find in religion or philosophy
the strength that they need to counteract their own
ineffectiveness, can still teach themselves by conscious
effort to get the best from their lives. As they do so,
many other things which have puzzled them become*

clear. But this book is not the history of the growth of an idea. It is intended to be a practical handbook for those who would like to escape from futility and begin to live happily and well.

CHAPTER I

WHY DO WE FAIL?

WITH the time and energy we spend in making failure a certainty we might have certain success.

A nonsensical paradox? No; fortunately it is a sober, literal truth, one which holds a great deal of promise.

Suppose a man had an appointment a hundred miles north of his home, and that if he kept it he would be sure of having health, much happiness, fair prosperity, for the rest of his life. He has just time enough to get there, just enough gas in his car. He drives out, but decides that it would be more fun to go twenty-five miles south before starting out in earnest.

That *is* nonsense! Yes, isn't it? The gas had nothing to do with it; Time had no preference as to how it would be spent; the road ran north as well as south, yet he missed his appointment. Now, if that man told us that, after all, he had quite enjoyed the drive in the wrong direction, that in some ways he found it pleasanter to drive with no objective than to try to keep a date, that he had had a touching glimpse of his old home by driving south, should we praise him for being properly philosophical about having lost his opportunity?

No, we should think he had acted like an imbecile. Even if he had missed his appointment by getting into a day-dream in which he drove automatically past a road-sign or two, we should still not absolve him. Or if he had arrived too late from having lost his way when he might have looked up his route on a good map and failed to do so before starting, we might commiserate with him, but we should indict him for bad judgment.

Yet when it comes to going straight to the appointments we make with ourselves and our own fulfillment, we all act very much like the hero of this silly fable: we drive the wrong

—14—

way. We fail where we might have succeeded by spending the same power and time.

Failure indicates that energy has been poured into the wrong channel. *It takes energy to fail.*

Now this is something which we seldom see at once. Because we commonly think of failure as the conventional opposite of success, we continue to make false antitheses of the qualities which attend success and failure. Success is bracing, active, alert; so the typical attitude of failure, we believe, must be lethargy, inertia, a supine position. True enough; but that does not mean that no energy is being used. Let any psychologist tell you how much energy a mature man must expend to resist motion. A powerful struggle must be waged against the forces of life and movement in order to remain inert, although this struggle takes place so far beneath the surface of our lives that we do not always become aware of it. Physical inaction is no true sign that life-force is not being burned away. So even the idler is using fuel while he dreams.

When failure comes about through devoting precious hours to time-killing pursuits, we can all see that energy is being diverted from its proper channel. But there are ways of killing time which do not look like dissipation. They can seem, on the contrary, like conscientious and dutiful hard work, they often draw praise and approval from onlookers, and arouse a sense of complacency in us. It is only by looking more closely, by discovering that this work gets us nowhere, that it both tires us and leaves us unsatisfied, that we see here again energy is being devoted to the pursuit of failure.

But why should this be so? Why, if, with the same energy we must use in any case, we might be succeeding, do we so seldom live the lives we hoped and planned to live? Why do we accomplish so little, and thwart ourselves senselessly? Why, when we start late, or run out of gas because of carelessness, or miss road-signs through day-dreaming, do we think we are being properly philosophical when we give ourselves and others excuses for failure which will not hold water? No one truly consoles himself by considering that a bird in the hand is worth two in the bush, that to travel hopefully is better than to arrive, that half-a-loaf is better than no bread. Such proverbs are the cynical distillation of experience, but they are nothing to live by. We deceive no one, although our compromises and excuses are accepted by our fellows as long as they are in the same boat. The successful man or woman listens to such whistling in the dark with amusement and incredulity, privately concluding that there is a great deal of hypocrisy loose in the world. He has the best of evidence that the rewards of well-directed activity far surpass all the by-products of failure, that one infinitesimal accomplishment in reality is worth a mountain of dreams.

Even as we tell of the compensations of failure we are not quite comfortable. We do not truly believe—although our proverbs sound as though we did—that one must choose either success *or* the good life. We know that those who succeed see the same sunsets, breathe

the same air, love and are loved no less than failures; and in addition they have something more: the knowledge that they have chosen to move in the direction of life and growth instead of acquiescing in death and decay. However we may talk, we know that Emerson was right when he wrote: "Success is constitutional; depends on a *plus* condition of mind and body, on power of work, on courage."

Then why do we fail? Especially, why do we *work hard* at failure?

Because, beside being creatures subject to the Will to Live and the Will to Power, we are driven by another will, the Will to Fail, or Die.

This is to many of us a novel idea. Of the Will to Live and the Will to Power we hear a great deal; our psychologies and philosophies make much of them. But the Will to Fail is more obscure, harder to observe at work. It takes as many forms as the Old Man of the Sea, and there are as many individual ways of failing—and failing "honorably" and successfully—as there are subdivisions of the psychological types. So it takes us unawares. We are not braced against it, being more used to thinking of failure as a shadow or phantom than a reality to be met and conquered, yet going in mortal fear of it all our lives.

To realize that there is this Will to Fail, or—which amounts to the same thing—this Will to Death, operative in our lives, that there is a down-dragging, devitalizing, frustrating current running counter to all the forces of health and growth in us, is the first step in turning from failure to success. We cannot begin by ignoring it, for then it can get in its subversive work most subtly. We must face it first, and then turn ourselves away from it.

It is possible to get back the energy that is now going into failure and use it to healthy ends. There are certain facts—plain, universal, psychological truths—which, when once seen, bring us to definite conclusions. From those conclusions we can make a formula on which to act. There is a simple, practical procedure which will turn us around and set our faces in the right direction. It is the formula, as we have said, on which, consciously or unconsciously, every successful person acts.

The procedure is simple, the first steps of putting it into practice so easy that those who prefer to dramatize their difficulties may refuse to believe that anything so uncomplicated could possibly help them. On the other hand, since it takes little time and soon brings its own evidence that, simple or not, its consequences are frequently amazing, it should be worth trying. A richer life, better work, the experience of success and its rewards: those ends are surely worth one experiment in procedure. All the equipment needed is imagination and the willingness to disturb old habit-patterns for a while, to act after a novel fashion long enough to finish one piece of work. How long that period is will vary, of course, with the work to be accomplished, and whether it is all dependent on oneself or of the unwieldier type which the executive and administrator know, where the factor of other human temperaments must be taken into account. In any case, some results from the experiment will be seen at once. Often these first results are so astonishing that to enumerate them here might alienate readers of a sober habit of mind. To hear of them before coming to them normally would be like hearing of miracles, and some of the effectiveness of the program might be lost by the intrusion of the very doubts we are out to banish.

Once more: however remarkable the results, the process is straightforward and uncomplicated. It is worth trying, for it has worked in hundreds of lives. It can work in any life that is not more truly dedicated to failure than to success.

CHAPTER II

THE WILL TO FAIL

Fʀᴏᴍ the disciples of Schopenhauer and
Freud, of Nietzsche and Adler, we have
all become conversant with such phrases as
the Will to Live and the Will to Power. These
phrases, representing—sometimes to the verge
of overstatement—drives of the organism
towards fulfillment and growth, correspond to
truths of experience with which each of us is
familiar. We have seen children struggle to
make themselves and their personalities felt;
as young people we have contended for a
chance to try our own emerging forces; after
long illness we have felt the tide of returning
strength in our veins. We know that any average man caught in unfortunate circumstances
will put up with poverty, distress, humiliation, with conditions which an onlooker will
sometimes consider as much worse than death;

and that only the presence of a will to continue living can account for the tenacity with which a man in such circumstances clings to the mere right to breathe and exist.

Furthermore, we first experience and then later turn to realize the process of growth in ourselves. The individual emerges from childhood into adolescence, from adolescence into maturity; and at each of these crises we find that the activities and interests of the old period are being replaced by those of the new, that Nature is preparing the organism for its new rôle in the world, is actually reconciling us to the new demands on us by showing us pleasures and rewards in the oncoming state which will replace those we must abandon.

But the idea of another will, a counterbalancing will, the Will to Fail, the Will to Death, is not so readily accepted. For a while it was one of the tenets of psycho-analysis, for instance, that no individual could actually imaginatively encompass the idea that he might *cease to be*. Even the death-dreams and suicide-threats of deeply morbid patients were held to be grounded solely in ideas of revenge: the explanation was that the patient thought of himself as living on, invisible, but able to see the remorse and regret caused by his death in those by whom he thought himself ill-treated.

Freud, indeed, analyzing shell-shocked patients after the War, issued a monograph in which he stated that he had occasionally found dreams that indicated sincere death-wishes. This monograph is full of some of the best of Freud's speculations and suggestions; but as for the appearance in popular psychologies of the idea that there could logically be a deathward current running through our lives, it is as though the thesis had never been suggested.

Yet death is as much a fact of experience as birth and growth; and if Nature prepares us for each new phase of life by closing off old desires and opening new vistas, it does not seem too difficult to think that we are, always, being slowly, gently reconciled to our eventual relinquishment of all we hold dear as living creatures. And withdrawal from struggle, abandonment of effort, releasing of desire and ambition would be normal movements in an organism which was being gently wooed away from its preoccupation with life.

It is for this reason that we are entitled to look upon the Will to Fail as a reality.

Now, if inertia, timorousness, substitute activity, effortless effort, quiescence, and resignation were found only at the end of life, or when we were drained by sickness or fatigue, if they never handicapped us when we should be in the full flood of our vital powers, there would be no reason at all for attacking this Will to Fail as if it were—as indeed it is—the arch-enemy of all that is good and effective in us. But when it appears in youth or full maturity it is as symptomatic of something wrong—deeply, internally wrong—with one's life as untimely drowsiness is symptomatic of ordinary bodily ill health.

And if it were easily seen for the black-hearted villain it is, when it arrives out of its due time, it would be easy to fight. But almost always we are well within its power before we do more than suspect rarely and vaguely that all is not as it should be with us. We are so accustomed to speak of failure, frustration, timidity, as negative things, that it is like being invited to fight windmills when we are urged to fight the symptoms of failure.

In youth we seldom recognize the symptoms in ourselves. We explain our reluctance to getting started as the natural timidity of the tyro; but the reluctance stays, the years go, and we wake in dismay to find that what was once a charming youthful diffidence in us is now something quite different, sickly and repellent. Or we find a convenient domestic situation to bear the brunt of excusing us for never having got to work in earnest. We could not leave this or that relative lonely and defenseless. Then the family grows, scatters, and we are left alone, the substitute activity at which we had been so busy is taken remorselessly away from us, and we are sick and terrified at the idea of turning back to take up the long-abandoned plans.

Or we have the best of all reasons for not doing as well as we might. Most of us are under the necessity of choosing between work and starvation, and the employment we were able to find when it was imperative that we should begin earning is not work for which we are ideally suited. When marriage and the raising of a family have been undertaken, the necessity is all the more urgent. We might be willing to wait through a few thin years if no one but ourselves would suffer, but to ask others to do so takes more selfishness, and more courage, than most of us can muster.

Especially in America, where marriages for love are the rule, most young people start out on their married life with little more than their health, youth, and intelligence as capital. We are accustomed to think of the European idea of asking a *dot*, a dower, from the bride's family as somehow ignoble and mercenary. Yet insisting on that little reserve fund of money with which to meet the demands of establishing a new household has much to recommend it, and the fact that we have no such custom in this country may be one reason why America, the much-vaunted Land of Opportunity, can show so many men and women of middle age wasting themselves in drudgery, filling positions which bring them no joy, and looking forward to a future which at its happiest promises years of monotony, and at its worst the nightmare of poverty-ridden unemployment.

This necessity to fall upon the first work we can find is alone enough to explain why so few of us ever manage to bring our plans to fruition. Often, at first, we have a firm intention of not losing sight of our real goal, in spite of the fact that we must make a living at uncongenial work. We plan to keep an eye on our ambitions, and to work at them by hook or crook—evenings, week-ends, on vacations. But the nine-to-five work is tiring and exacting; it takes superhuman strength of character to go on working alone when the rest of the

world is at play, and when we have never had
any evidence that we should be successful if
we continued, anyway. And so without realizing it we are swept into the current of the Will
to Fail. We are still moving, and we do not
see that our motion is down-stream.

Most of us disguise our failure in public;
we disguise it most successfully from ourselves. It is not hard to ignore the fact that
we are doing much less than we are able to
do, very little of what we had planned even
modestly to accomplish before a certain age,
and never, probably, all that we had hoped.
One reason it is so easy to deceive ourselves is
that somewhere along the way we seem
silently to enter into a sort of gentleman's
agreement with our friends and acquaintances. "Don't mention my failure to me,"
we tacitly plead, "and I will never let the hint
that you are not doing quite all I should
expect of you cross my lips."

This tactful silence is seldom broken in
youth or in the early middle years. Until
then, the convention is that at any moment

we may get into our stride. A little later and the silence is relaxed. There comes a time when it is safe to smile ruefully and admit that the hopes we went out to meet the world with were too high and much too rosy, particularly those hopes we had held for our own perform- ance. In the fifties—and sometimes earlier— it is usually safe enough to do a little disarm- ing and semi-humorous grumbling; after all, few of our contemporaries are in a position to say "Why can't you start now?" And yet some of the greatest work in the world, many of the world's irreplaceable masterpieces, were done by men and women well past what we too superficially consider their prime.

So we slip through the world without mak- ing our contribution, without discovering all that there was in us to do, without using the most minute fraction of our abilities, either native or acquired. If we manage to be fairly comfortable, to get some respect and admira- tion, a taste of "a little brief authority" and some love, we think we have made a good bargain, we acquiesce in the Will to Fail. We

CHAPTER III

VICTIMS OF THE WILL TO FAIL

IF the Will to Fail announced its presence with symptoms as uniform and unmistakable as those which indicate measles or a bad cold, it would probably have been eradicated, or a technique for combatting it would have been worked out, long ago.

But unfortunately its symptoms are varied and legion. If you were to drag a dining, dancing, theatre-going, middle-aged metropolitan playboy away from his merry-go-round and introduce him to an unshaven, ill-clad crackerbox philosopher dreaming in the sun, saying "I want you two to know each other; you have so much in common," you would be thought mad, yet you would be right. The dreaming idler, the introvert, and the dancing extrovert

—at the antipodes from the point of view of worldly circumstance—are motivated by the same impulse; unconsciously they are both trying to fail.

Their lives have a common denominator. "Do not act as if you had a thousand years to live," Marcus Aurelius warned himself in his maxims. All those in the grip of the Will to Fail act as if they had a thousand years before them. Whether they dream or dance, they spend their precious hours as though the store of them were inexhaustible.

But since there are as many ways of failing as there are divisions and subdivisions of the psychological types, we often do not recognize the presence of the Will to Fail in others or in ourselves. Here are a few of the innumerable ways of "acting as though you had a thousand years to live":

There are, for instance, those who sleep from two to six hours a day more than they need to sleep to keep in perfect physical health. In any individual case, unless the sleeping-hours far exceed the normal quota, it is very hard to be sure one has not to do with merely an unusually long sleeper. But when the note of compulsion enters, one can be sure of having found a true victim of failure. Those who are bad-tempered or only half alive if an early bedtime must be postponed, those who anxiously count each morning the exact number of hours spent in sleep the night before, mourning inconsolably any interruption, every hour of insomnia, every untimely doorbell, are looking to sleep for more than its normal restorative function. When an adult extends even this, making a nap or two a day a matter of routine, the diagnosis becomes simple.

Next, still among the inconspicuous failures, the "introverts," are the waking sleepers: persons who allow some activity to pass before them almost without participation, or indulge in time-killing pursuits in which they take only the most minor and unconstructive parts: the solitaire-players, the pathological bookworms, the endless crossword-puzzlers, the jigsaw puzzle contingent. The line between recreation and obsession is not hard to see once we know it is there.

Easiest of all to recognize as lovers of failure are the heavy drinkers. A volume could be written on them, but too many volumes have. Where drinking is so constant as to bring on a waking sleep, or, deeper, a kind of death in life, the presence of the Will to Fail is obvious to any observer. But there are thousands who show the symptoms in so faint a form that they pass almost unnoticed: all those who drink knowing that it means a bad morning the next day, a vague and woolly approach to every problem until the effects have passed off; those to whom any drinking means physical discomfort, whether acute or trifling. Anyone who has learned to expect these consequences and yet continues to lay himself open to them stands convicted of the desire to handicap himself, at least to that extent. It makes very little difference what the drink in question may be. If coffee disturbs you, if you cannot digest milk, and you nevertheless continue to drink it, you may escape the disapproval which is meted out to the highball drinker, but you are in the same class. And, plainly, unwise eating comes under the same head.

Turning to the active type, it may be said that the extroverts who pursue failure as their primary career find so many ways of doing it that the attempt to tabulate them all would be hopeless. But, as examples, there are the relentless movie- and theatre-goers, the nightly dancers, all those who count the day lost which has not a tea or dinner or cocktail-party in it. . . . No, of course there is nothing against relaxation and recreation when they are really called for, after a period of contributory activity. But those who enter an objection to this classification too early and too angrily, crying that one *must* have recreation, give themselves dead away as setting an abnormal value on release.

Then there are the half-and-half failures, difficult to place, such as the embroiderers and knitters, although it is only fair to say here that sometimes a light task calling for only manual dexterity may go on while the mind is usefully engaged in solving a real problem. Complete honesty with oneself is all that is necessary to discover whether the rhythmical activity is being used in one way or the other. If a dull stupor sets in, or if, on the other hand, the work is just elaborate enough, calls for just enough conscious attention so that no automatic rhythm can be established, then it is rare indeed that this kind of motion can be put in the category of true creative activity, or that of being accessory to creative action.

As to aimless conversationalists, we can more easily see that others fall in that group than that we are included ourselves. Sometimes we are startled into realizing that we have repeated the same anecdote to the same friend, and for a few days go warily. That is a minor slip. No reminiscent ring, no forced smile on our auditor's lips will stop us when we are habitually marking time with words— when we have the same unevolving round of topics, the same opinions to repeat mechanically, the same half-aimless observations to make on the same recurring situations, the same automatic indignation at the same old abuses, the same illustrations to prove the same points, and a few lukewarm arguments to bolster up what may once have been opinions but are now seldom more than prejudices.

Sometimes we ride a verbal mannerism so hard that a hearer objects irritably. (Suggestions for overcoming such mannerisms will be given later; here we are only considering the way in which they unconsciously betray in us the presence of a Will to Fail.) It is probably a great piece of luck to rouse a friend to this extent. If you learn with shocking suddenness that you are forever saying "I mean," "Of course," "I imagine," "Do you see?" "You know," "As a matter of fact," you are likely to listen to your own voice for a period and discover that not only do these tag-words occur over and over in your conversation, but that there is nothing particularly fresh or valuable about the ideas they have served to embellish. Here, as in the other categories, it is very easy to see that there is something wrong when one meets gross examples of the difficulty; an hysterical talker is obviously mentally ill. But that there are subtler forms of the same trouble, often hidden for years because we do our repeating to constantly changing audiences, seldom dawns on us.

There are still more obscure and unnoticeable ways of falling victim to the Will to Fail, ways to which introverts and extroverts are almost equally susceptible. Consider the innumerable persons, for instance, who deliberately undertake work which calls for only a small part of their abilities and training, and who then drive themselves relentlessly, exhausting themselves over useless details. There are the takers of eternal post-graduate courses, turning up on the campus year after year like so many Flying Dutchmen. There are the "devoted" daughters and sons and mothers and wives (fathers are seldom found here, for some reason, although there may be an occasional husband) who pour out their lives into the lives of other adults, but whose offering, since they have never truly developed what was most valuable in themselves, adds no richness and only unimportant comfort to the objects of their "self-sacrifice." There are those who undertake a task known by them to be beyond their powers, or engage in a specious "research" problem: there is a man in New York, for example, who has been gathering biographical details about an obscure Italian statesman since his sophomore year in college. This pseudo-biographer is now in his late forties, and not one word of that definitive *Life* had been written.

Perhaps the greatest class of all those whose goal is failure is that of the Universal Charmers.

When you find yourself in the presence of more charm than the situation calls for, you are safe in saying to yourself, "Ah, a failure!" This is no diatribe against genuine warmheartedness, against friendliness, or true sweetness of character. We are talking now about the Harold Skimpoles of the world, about the cajolling, winsome adult, either man or woman, who insists on being accepted by his contemporaries as just a great, big, delightful child—irresponsible, perhaps, not very thoughtful, but so exceedingly lovable, even to strangers! There are the whimsical teases and the humorous complainers, and if they are good to look at, quick-witted or amusing, they are more likely than not to be successful in arousing a momentary indulgence, a tolerant tenderness. It is only in retrospect that one realizes there was no valid reason for the moment's emotion. A healthy adult does not need the tenderness or indulgence of every casual acquaintance. Except for a guilty conscience, no one would ever dream of making a play for this kind of response. These victims are under the hard necessity of working at charm as convicts work at stone-crushing; they must go on being more and more charming to offset their waning attractions, or face the truth—admit that they have not adequately discharged their responsibilities. As long as their inadequacy is never seen except mirrored in the indulgent eyes of another they can go on without admitting the fact that they are failing. So on they go, cheating their way through life—unless by good fortune they can come to see who really suffers most from the exercise of their charm.

So there are all these ways, and innumerable others, of filling one's time with seemingly purposeless activity, or a falsely purposeful routine, and they are all the result of submitting to the Will to Fail.

For, remember, these activities are only *apparently* purposeless. There is in every case a deep intention, which may be stated in many ways.

We may say that the most obvious intention is to beguile the world into believing that we are living up to our fullest capacity. This is particularly true of those cases where the outward life is full of a thousand little matters, or one big job of drudgery conscientiously done. No one, surely, could ask us to do *more* than we are doing! Are we not plainly so busy that we have not one minute or a grain of strength to do anything more? Is it not our duty to do the dull, insignificant, unsatisfying task thoroughly? Those are questions which only the individual can answer honestly for himself, usually in the hours of insomnia or convalescence, when the mind which is usually so engrossed about trivial affairs finds time to stop and consider. In the long run it makes little difference how cleverly others are deceived; if we are not doing what we are best equipped to do, or doing well what we have undertaken as our *personal* contribution to the world's work, at least by way of an earnestly followed avocation, there will be a core of unhappiness in our lives which will be more and more difficult to ignore as the years pass.

The fritterers and players and the drudging workers are bent mainly on deceiving themselves, on filling every nook and cranny of their waking hours so that there is no spot where a suspicion of futility can leak through. And at night, of course, they are either still hard at play or too exhausted to consider realities. Yet such victims present a dreadful spectacle when once they are plainly seen—seen as insane misers, stuffing a senseless accumulation of trash, odds and ends of sensations, experiences, fads and enthusiasms, synthetic emotions, into the priceless coffer of their one irreplaceable lifetime.

Whatever the ostensible purpose may be, it is plain that one motive is at work in all these cases: *the intention, often unconscious, to fill life so full of secondary activities or substitute activities that there will be no time in which to perform the best work of which one is capable.*

The intention, in short, is to fail.

CHAPTER IV

THE REWARDS OF FAILURE

ABSURD as it may seem at first consideration that anyone would solemnly enter into even an unconscious conspiracy to fail, it is a matter of observation that there is hardly one person in a hundred who does not, in some fashion, deliberately cripple and thwart himself. To understand why this should be so it is necessary to examine for a chapter what may be called, without paradox, the rewards of failure.

The recent widespread interest in all branches of psychology has accustomed us to accepting an idea which, when first offered, seemed laughable: that we are all, at some level, engaged most of the time in revery. We dream either consciously or unconsciously, awake or asleep, of a situation in which we feel we should be happier than we are in real life. Occasionally some childish idea of happiness or success crops up to confuse or hamper us in the business of adult living. Sometimes the dream is of a life of luxurious idleness, the childish Unconscious determined on refusing to leave the safe shelter of the nursery, where all wants were remedied as soon as felt, where warmth and food and love were given freely and unearned. As Emerson wrote, long before we had any technical vocabulary to express that backward-turning revery, long before we knew of "fixations" or of "narcissism," "We do not believe there is any force in today to rival or recreate that beautiful Yesterday. We linger in the ruins of the old tent where once we had bread and shelter." To some extent this is true of all of us, but less true of the happy and successful adult than of others.

At other times, ludicrously enough, the life-wasting revery is about success: the mild man is a Napoleon of war or finance, the mouse-like woman a siren. If reality never broke in upon such revery, the dreamer might be happier, self-absorbed in his silent tale-spinning, than if he were to find himself in a position to realize some part of it. Such revery is in itself compensation for a life of dull routine or uneventful monotony. But, the world being what it is, the dreamer must live, for part of his time at least, in the cold atmosphere of fact. This is no Land of Cockaigne that we inhabit: roast pigs do not run about crying "Eat me!" Fruit does not fall from the trees into our mouths. However blissful the day-dream we entertain, we must wake from it sometimes and struggle with the hard conditions of real living.

The inveterate dreamer will struggle only just as much as he need, and no more. He will do anything half-heartedly to get his bread and butter. Then, when his daily task is over, he will be back at his dreams again, whether he realizes it or not. He succeeds at only one thing: in clearing away a little space, gaining each day a few hours of free time, for just one purpose—to go on wasting his life. But his dream is happy. It is, for him, a true compensation for his failure in every other relation, and so he continues in it. Yet, since after all happiness is the true goal, he is deluded by not realizing that the smallest success in reality brings with it more happiness than years of revery.

Nevertheless it is important to remember that the rewards of failure are real in their own sphere, for otherwise we will not brace ourselves to fight them adequately; and there are other rewards of failure besides dreams.

Consider, for instance, that if you try for anything just enough to give yourself some justification for saying that you *have* tried, you can fold your hands for the rest of your days. You can say humbly that you were tried and found wanting in those qualities which make for real success. This is rather a rare remark, but one of those which can be heard now and then from older failures, usually in a humorously deprecating tone. It will sound very honest and touching; and there is no earthly way in which it can be proved against the complainant that his statement is not fully true.

He has saved himself a lifetime of effort by *some* means, nevertheless. If you join this group you can watch the struggles of others with an eye half-amused, half-envious, enjoying the results of their successes, but perhaps even more—human nature being what it is— the spectacle of those who fail, and who take up their onlookers' positions beside you.

Then, "Mankind is very superficial and dastardly," as Franklin said. "They begin upon a thing, but meeting with a difficulty, they fly from it discouraged"; and why not, asks the Unconscious, when you can try, stop, and feel for the rest of your life that if you had tried *just once more* you would have made the grade? You can thereupon become a dilettante or amateur, frightfully hard to please by those who go on working, severest of all critics either professional or unprofessional, possessor of some inner knowledge, and able to hint at standards of excellence untouched by those who are still out trying to run the dusty race; standards so marvellous, so unattainable, that failure to reach them is more honorable, you may imply, than another man's easy success. With not one thing completed, the acclaim you *might* have received, the enormous financial coup you *might* have brought off, the masterpiece you *might* have accomplished, can assume in your revery, and in the eyes of those who will accept your version of things, almost more importance than the real success would have had.

Or you can become an abettor and sustainer of more persistent workers and artists, and perhaps that is the friendliest failure, the most successful failure, of all.

But notice that in all these cases you will at the very least have avoided the struggle, the pain, the humiliations that attend outward activity. You will never have to see the object you slaved to bring into being despised or misunderstood. You will never have to feel the rancour of those whom you necessarily surpassed in competition; you will never have to stand the cut of adverse criticism. You will never have to become aware of the malice of those who envy any success, however trivial.

You will never have to back your opinions by argument when you are tired and would rather rest for new effort. Or, far deeper and more vital pain, you will never see the discrepancy between the finished work you can do and the work as you had hoped to do it. There is always that discrepancy to keep the honest worker really humble.

These matters of discomfort and pain evaded are important to notice, for when we come to examine the reasons why we so often choose to fail rather than to succeed, they will prove very illuminating. So it is worth understanding that *if you fail you are rewarded* by not running the risk of getting hot and tired and discouraged, or sharp-tempered when your co-workers or your materials, whatever they are, seem more refractory than usual. If someone else does excellently in the line you had dreamed of for yourself, you can always believe that, if you had really tried again, you could have surpassed him.

And then, if you can remain inconspicuous, you will not have the experience of outstripping someone you love. This is, perhaps, most commonly the woman's Reward of Failure, although the children of distinguished parents or the disciples of outmoded masters in any line also know it. Still, it is only right to say that many who dread the experience of causing pain to another are never called upon to meet it; they failed to take into account the generosity of love. So it is often an excuse for not working that is at the root of this inaction, too, not a real matter of compromising with ambition in order to keep a vital relationship unspoiled.

By failing one escapes much gossip and incomprehension, the semi-scandalous talk which most often springs up about those who succeed. To dread this immoderately is neurotic, but this dread does often act as a deterrent to many a success. All vital persons are the target of the curiosity of those who are not vital; but the few whose opinions concern you will know the truth, and the others are of no importance. Yet many withdraw from active life, not to take up an intenser inner life, but merely to avoid the vulgar curiosity of the crowd.

And then, if you have failed not too awkwardly, you are usually more delightful as a companion than a better worker. Those who reach real success are likely to be constant workers. Even in their hours of recreation they frequently are preoccupied with some element of the thing they are engaged in doing. The successful man has less free time, and observes more punctiliously his self-set hours for withdrawing from companionship, than the failure. He can seldom be counted on for impromptu gaieties, since he is not unconsciously intent on finding any escape at all from the unsatisfactory conditions of his life. And, since he has none of the deep interior guilt which haunts the one who knows he is failing, he is under no compulsion to be winning. He reserves his humor and charm, his emotion and indulgence, for those whose lives are closely bound up with his by his own choice. So, except among his real intimates, he may have the name of being gruff and unapproachable, or too coolly civil. As long as you cannot bear the notion that there is a creature under heaven who can regard you with an indifferent, an amused or hostile eye, you will probably see to it that you continue to fail with the utmost charm.

Perhaps it will be helpful to look for a while at three lives in which the Will to Fail was at work. In every case the onlooker would see a life of considerable activity, such obvious activity that he would at first glance be likely to agree with the victims that they were in the grip of a perverse fate. On closer examination, each failure will be seen to be by no means determined by any factor outside the individual character. Each of these persons had within himself or herself the abilities necessary to make a full, happy, productive life; each spent what energy he had on defeating his ostensible intention: one saw her mistake and rectified it, one died without facing the truth about his wasted talents. The third is still struggling with his problem, as far from success as ever, though his name is well known.

Case 1 is that of a woman, left a widow while she was still very young. She came of a scholarly family, and had been a brilliant student at college. With the little money left to care for herself and her small daughter, she returned to the campus to take degrees as Master of Arts and Doctor of Philosophy in preparation for a career as an educator. Actually (as she found to her astonishment when her difficulties became so great as to force her to seek advice) she delighted in being a student again, in continuing to live in the condition of a child in an adult world, and therefore strung out her period of preparation as long as she dared. After her Ph.D. was earned, she made what looked to herself and her friends like a good honest effort to find a suitable niche for herself. *Only* she invariably engaged in wrangling acrimoniously with those who would have to be her superiors, and always about some rather remarkable and original economic ideas of her own. These ideas had nothing whatever to do with the subject she was to teach; their acceptance or rejection

by the entire world would not have made one
grain of difference in the class-room work
which she was called on to perform; but by
making an issue of having her absurd and
quixotic ideas taken seriously by her co-
workers, she brought about—each time she
found a position—a situation in which she was
distinctly disliked by the very persons on
whose good will she was dependent.

She went from one post to another, never
holding one longer than the year for which
she had contracted. She was a good teacher, a
well-informed student, and she had much to
give, but she carefully saw to it that she would
never be in a position to work very hard for
very long. Her hopes of a professorship faded.
She went from good colleges steadily down-
grade to obscure little schools, and as she
slipped steadily down she worked out a philosophy which reconciled her to her steady
decline. She held that we all live much too
luxuriously, and put too high a value on becoming clothes, good food, and comfort. At
last she reached the place where she felt justi-

fied in taking an apartment in a tenement district of a large city. Her defiant self-justification broke down, however, when it came to inviting friends to visit her. She grew more and more solitary, more and more eccentric, her running fire of bravado continuing all the while.

Fortunately for her, her one child was a girl, and a girl who grew up to be extremely bright and attractive. She was quite unimpressed by her mother's pseudo-philosophy; she knew that she was being handicapped at every turn by the oddness of their living and dressing, and as she emerged into adolescence she began to fight for a more reasonable life, a suitable background. Matters came to such a pass that either the mother had to take cognizance of the girl's objections or lose her daughter. All the efforts to correct her false position which she made by herself were unavailing. She still brought about the old wrangles whenever possible, she still held the unsatisfactory position to which she had dropped only on tolerance and because she had come to accept a very small salary, in spite of her training and ability.

When at last she sought help from a psychologist she discovered to her dumbfounded astonishment that she had actually thrown all her energy into failing. Unconsciously she had resented having to go out into the world to work. She wanted to remain either a child or become again a cherished and petted wife. Her wrangles had been, as the analysts say, "over-determined": they were intended partly to make it certain that she would be discharged so that work would become impossible, partly to engage the attention of men. Since she could not acknowledge to herself that she was cold-bloodedly "husband-hunting," she had fallen on the technique—quite as effective in challenging attention as being charming—of starting quarrels. She had a long, hard pull to right the situation she had brought upon herself, but she was eventually successful.

Case 2 is such a one as can be found in almost every town and village in the country, a failure of the sort that is not only treated tenderly, but often looked upon as being in some vague way much nobler and finer than any success. It was that of a man with a good mind, noted for his integrity and yet not without a vein of good Yankee ingenuity. He lived and died in the small town of his birth; a rather ugly little manufacturing town. Not because he loved it loyally and wanted nothing better; his reading was always of travel and adventure, and he continually spoke wistfully of countries and places he had never seen. Not that he had no opportunity—opportunity came and tried to hound him into activity. He was the manager of a branch store of a large business, and so satisfactory at it that he was offered a similar position in a larger city, at a correspondingly better salary. He accepted with joy; then within two days he wrote a letter saying that he had reconsidered, that he did not believe that he could fill the better position. His timidity grew on him. A few years later he was combatting every improved method that his firm tried to introduce, afraid to try the new ways. A little later he was such an obstructionist that his firm retired him on a minute pension, and he became the town's lovable homespun philosopher.

A senator spoke movingly at his funeral; his fellow townsmen were inconsolable. . . . Perhaps it is deplorably callous to point out that his wife had preceded him to the grave by ten years, worn out with overwork; that one son had no education beyond what he could get at the village school, although he had as good a mind as his father; that the other son had to work his way through college, thus dividing his energy and strength (for it is only one more fallacy of the American creed that to work one's way through college is the ideal way of getting an education), that his daughter had taken refuge in a loveless marriage from a home that had never had enough of the ordinary comforts or attractions.

Let us be perfectly plain about one point: to hold that honest success is in some way ignoble is one of two things—pretense or cant.

There is a tyrannical effort to impose this fallacy on us, arising perhaps from a confusion
of the mere word "success" with the idea of a
great fortune arrived at by fair means or foul.
But that there is anything ignoble in accomplishing well what one sets out to do, and in
receiving in return rewards in the shape,
sometimes of the approval of one's peers,
sometimes the quiet knowledge that the world
is richer for one's contribution, or sometimes
in money paid out gladly for an object or
services fully worth the price to the purchaser
—such an idea is nonsense, and the very opposite of what it is usually claimed to be,
"philosophical."

William Ernest Hocking, in his excellent
book, *Human Nature and Its Remaking,* has
this to say on that very point: "If command of
the fruits of the earth is the normal and des-
tined position for man, why should one who
has achieved such a position, and in so doing
has shown large powers of one kind or another, not receive the recognition that he, in
so far, has succeeded? It is a man's work to

make a fortune, and under normal circumstances a measure of ability."

Many who know Case 3 by his name would protest loudly at his appearance here incognito as an illustration of the Will to Fail at work. He is a writer, and the son of a writer. From the first he has been under such a fortunate star that he knows almost nothing of the long struggle for recognition which is so often the prelude to a literary career. Nevertheless, at one and the same time he lives in terror of failure and in the grip of an instinct which seems to drive him in that direction. He will not work until he is desperate for money; then he will write like mad, tiring himself till he is poisoned with fatigue, and acts afterwards like a convalescent. Trying to overcome this bad working-habit under the advice of a psychiatrist, he attempted to work, more than once, when there was no urgent necessity for money. In those circumstances he invariably turned out stories which were unacceptable until rewritten. The world knows nothing, of course, of those wasted ef-

forts, that time spent in the disheartening re-
visions which he is constantly called on to
do. Each time this occurs his career seems
drearier and less glamorous to him, his belief
that he can eventually write a book he will not
be ashamed to sign with his name grows
dimmer.

Here again analysis brought some illumination as to the unconscious reason for this
action, and again the tendency to do haphazard and unsatisfactory work was over-
determined: there was on the one hand a
dread of surpassing his illustrious father at
the same profession, on the other the sly unconscious notion that if the stories he seemed
to slave over were rejected he would not have
to work at all, and would be free to dream
through his life in his own way. For the Unconscious always refuses to understand that
reality must be taken into account, refuses to
admit that "Work or die" is the rule the average mortal must live by.

Yet this tormented man recurrently has an
experience which might, if he could compre-

hend it, show him the way out of his dilemma: when he is at last desperate for money, when he cannot go any longer on credit or the indulgence of his friends, or his reputation, when, in short, he has the courage of desperation, he writes material which is immediately accepted. Instead of drawing the workable conclusion from this fact, he has made it an item of superstition: only work done, as he says, "at the thirteenth hour," is ever lucky for him! So he continues on his treadmill.

Now, in each of these cases, failure, or comparative failure, brought its reward with it: escape from adult effort and time to waste in day-dreaming. Only in those cases where frustration was more painful than success was there any attempt to reshape the life-pattern. Do you feel that obviously those who waste life in this way are at least mildly insane? We all make similar difficulties for ourselves, avoid work, miss opportunities. Have you ever looked back and thought, "If I had done this or that five years ago I'd be better off now?" But the opportunity was there; why didn't

you see it? Are you sure that you are not closing your eyes at this moment to one which
you will see later in retrospect? Is the Will
to Fail not operating in your own life every
day?

Yet the rewards of success are so immeas-
urably more worth having. Once more, the
smallest task well done, the smallest object,
out there in the world where it would not
have been if you had not acted, brings in a
moment more satisfaction than the failure
knows in a lifetime. The knowledge that one
is being tried by a real scale and not by the
shifting standards of revery is like having land
underfoot after weeks of drifting at sea. Only
those who are at work on the best they can do
are free from the danger of panic-stricken
awakening to reality—awakening sometimes
so late that the very habits and attitudes of
normality are forgotten.

And, beside the innumerable purely sub-
jective advantages, there are the rich objective rewards. A dream-picture brings no
buyer, a dream-plan no dividends, a fantasied

book is followed by no royalty statements. Crass as this may sound in a world which spends a great deal of its breath in persuading futilitarians that they have chosen the better part, it is the literal truth and stands for a truth still greater. Fantasy may call the grapes of reality sour, but those who have tasted them know at last a dependable delight.

CHAPTER V

RIGHTING
THE DIRECTION

In spite of the Will to Fail, in spite of the Rewards of Failure, success is the normal aim of man, his proper objective. Energy is correctly used not by spending it to hold ourselves inactive, nor by spurring ourselves to unproductive, sterile activity, but only when it is at the service of the maturest and most comprehensive idea of ourselves that we can arrive at.

What this highest idea is will vary from individual to individual, and will expand with growth. No outsider can dictate another's private definition of success. It may, it often does, include some recognition from one's fellows, and greater financial rewards; on the other hand, it may not. Many a researcher in

the sciences would consider himself fully successful (and would be right), if he added one
minute fact to the mass of accumulating details on which science must proceed, if he took
one item out of the realm of hypothesis and
speculation and placed it in its proper relation
to the mass of known truths. His name might
never be known by those outside his science;
it might be quite obscure even within his own
field. He would nevertheless have attained the
goal for which he was working if he accomplished that which he himself set out to do.

The actress who reaches the top of her art
is as successful as the mother who raises a
large and healthy family—but not more so. A
priest or minister immersed in the care of his
parish lives as successful a life as the genius
whose name is known by most of his contemporaries. Another's ideal of success may have
so little in common with our own that we are
quite blind as to what he can see in the career
he has chosen, but unless we are totally unimaginative we know, when we see him living
responsibly, effectively, usefully, happily,

making the most of his advantages and gifts, that we are dealing with a successful man.

To offer too circumscribed a definition of success would defeat the purpose of this book. Much of our distrust of the word, as it is, comes from not realizing the infinitely exten- sive range of possible "successes." Each of us, usually by late adolescence, has a mass of knowledge about himself, which—if we took the counsel "Know thyself" seriously—could be examined and considered until the individ- ual's ideal of the good life would emerge from it plainly. It ought to be part of education to see that each child should understand the necessity of finding this clue to his future, and be shown that it is sometimes thrown into con- fusion by hero-worship, or by the erroneous notion that what is an item in the success of one must be present in the success of each of us. Still, in spite of confusion, false starts, the taking over of the ambitions of a parent or teacher for ourselves instead of finding our own, most of us do arrive in the early twenties knowing what we are best fitted to do, or

could do best if we had the training and opportunity.

It is worth noting carefully that unless you
have allowed yourself to overestimate your
character grossly, your own success-idea is
within the region of those things which can
be brought about. Usually, far from over-
rating our abilities, we do not understand how
great they are. The reason for this under-
estimation of ourselves will be considered
later, but it is well to realize that few except
the truly insane believe themselves suited for
careers far beyond their full powers.

The next point to understand is that in
these pages we are not talking about success
of any secondary or metaphorical sort. Your
idea of what is success for you is not here to
be replaced by another high-sounding, "ideal-
istic" compromise. You are not being ex-
horted, once more, to lower your hopes and
then find that you can easily reach the simpler
standard. Such programs are only temporiz-
ing with failure. On the contrary, the more
vividly you can present to yourself the orig-

inal picture of the goal you once hoped to be able to reach, the better your chances are of attaining it.

Now, having examined the currents in our nature which lead us to acquiesce in failure, understanding that, if we allow it to happen, we can be carried unprotestingly down in the deathward direction, let us see what is operating *immediately* to keep us from the healthy efforts we must make to succeed.

To do so we must turn to a subject which is in some disrepute today: hypnotism. For many reasons, some excellent but others suspiciously weak, hypnotism is a subject which is seldom studied nowadays. If you have never had occasion to read a sound book on the subject, it may seem to you that some of the feats claimed for hypnotized persons cannot possibly have been done. There is some likelihood, however, that you have read at least one book on autosuggestion, the method of healing which was so popular about a decade ago, and autosuggestion is one of the by-products of the nineteenth-century study of hypnotism.

But few readers today know of the work, for instance, of Esdaile in India in the middle 1800's: of the surgical operations he performed painlessly on hundreds of patients, of his comments on the rapid recovery of those who had felt no pain during the operation— an early contribution to the theory of the deleterious effects of "surgical shock." The work of Braid and Bernheim is almost unknown, and Mesmer, who combined a fantastic theory with a mass of arrestingly effective experiments, is now looked on mainly as a quack.

There is no doubt that hypnotism is in its present disrepute partly because its early practitioners could not refrain from premature and fantastic theorizing, and because it became connected in the minds of the public with such subjects as "spirit-rappings" and "slate-writing" mediums, many of whom were later exposed as tricksters. Possible experimenters were alienated from the subject because it was offered to the world with such unnecessary accompaniments as the hypothe-

ses about "odic fluid" and "animal magne-
tism"—explanations which explained nothing.
In addition to these prejudicial theories, experiments in anæsthesia by the use of chloroform and ether were proceeding in the same
years. Insensitiveness to pain reached by
hypnosis was uncertain and presented many
difficulties: not everyone was hypnotizable,
and, even more important, not every physician was able to hypnotize. Inevitably, the
more certain form of attaining anæsthetiza-
tion through the use of chloroform and ether
was the practice which became accepted. The
study of hypnotism, which many acute ob-
servers of the middle and late nineteenth cen-
tury believed to be the first step towards the
freeing of mankind from physical suffering,
as well as the overcoming of many temperamental difficulties and the cure of many vices,
fell into a decline. With the emergence of the
psycho-analytic theory, the defeat of hypnotism—at least for our day—was cemented.

Now, although the formula that we are
about to consider has in it no trace of auto-

hypnotism, it is still possible to learn from the despised procedure what it is that defeats us in our efforts to be effective. Consider for a moment the successes of a good hypnotist with a good subject: they sound utterly beyond nature, and for that very reason we have not learned from them all we might garner. One man, ordinarily suffering from vertigo at even a slight eminence, when hypnotized can walk a very narrow plank at a great height. Another, looking slight and delicate, can lift a dead weight. A stammerer can be commanded to give a fervid oration, and will do so without showing a trace of the speech-defect which hampers him in his normal state. Perhaps one of the most remarkable cases is one cited by F. W. H. Myers in his chapter on hypnotism in *Human Personality:* a young actress, an understudy, called upon suddenly to replace the star of her company, was sick with apprehension and stage-fright. Under light hypnosis she performed with competence and brilliance, and won great applause; but it was long before she was able to act her parts without the aid of the hypnotist, who stationed himself in her dressing-room. (Later in this same case the phenomenon of "post-hypnotic suggestion" began to be observed, and the foundations of the Nancy School of auto-suggestion, of which Coué is the most famous contemporary associate, were laid.)

In the same chapter in which he quotes the remarkable case of the actress, Myers made a theorizing comment which is of immense value to everyone who hopes to free himself of his bondage to failure. He points out that the ordinary shyness and tentativeness with which we all approach novel action is entirely removed from the hypnotized subject, who consequently acts instead with precision and self-confidence.

Now the removal of shyness, or mauvaise honte (he wrote), *which hypnotic suggestion can effect, is in fact* a purgation of memory— *inhibiting the recollection of previous failures, and setting free whatever group of aptitudes is for the moment required.*

There is the clue. No sentence was ever

more packed with rich implications for those who are in earnest about re-orienting their lives towards success.

It has become a commonplace to say that we learn by "trial and error." We learn by discovering that one course of action does not bring about the end we had in view; we try again, and perhaps many times, until we find the procedure which accomplishes our intention. We then adopt the last term in this series of acts.

That is the mental picture we make of the "trial-and-error" method of learning. Roughly it is right, but it omits to emphasize one element of the process which, although we may not dwell upon it intentionally, is never forgotten by the Unconscious: the element of pain. We believe, or speak and write as though we believed, that the one success remains as the total residue of the series of attempts, and that it cancels from our minds all the failures which went before it. We do not take into account the tremendous importance to our future conduct of those discarded trials which ended in failure. We succeeded at last, it is true; but meanwhile we experienced failure, sometimes ridicule, sometimes real pain, sometimes grave humiliation. We by no means retain in our memories only the item of the final success, nor does the success operate to make the failures and pain unimportant to our Unconscious.

The Unconscious dreads pain, humiliation, fatigue; it bends its efforts even more ceaselessly to the end of avoiding pain than it does to the procuring of positive pleasures. So we are faced with a fact which at once accounts for much of the inactivity, the inertia, to which we succumb at moments when positive action would be to our advantage: *that rather than face the mere possibility of pain we will not act at all.*

Rather than revive the memory of our early failures, let alone run the risk of hurting ourselves anew, we will *unconsciously* decide to remain inactive, or we will choose to do something easier than we should attempt, or we will start on a program and carry it near the spot where we were hurt before, and there find any excuse to beat a hasty retreat, leaving the work undone, the reward ungathered. The childish Unconscious wins: at least we were not bruised again in an already tender spot.

It is utterly illogical, of course; in order to avoid a trivial discomfort we roll up a great account of failure to wound us in the future, we miss opportunity after opportunity which may never come again, we expose ourselves to far greater pain than that we manage to avoid. But at least the memory of that early humiliation can sleep, or only turn restlessly, half-awakened.

Now, if that is true—and only a little self-analysis will prove that it is true—how convenient it would be if each of us could carry a hypnotist about, to cast his spell whenever we had to get to work! How marvellous if each of us could have his own private Svengali! Impossible, of course; and, more than that, undesirable. Fortunately, it is not at all necessary to be put under the sway of another's

will in order to do our own work. The solu-
tion is far simpler. All that is necessary to
break the spell of inertia and frustration is
this:

. *Act as if it were impossible to fail.*

That is the talisman, the formula, the command of right-about-face which turns us from
failure towards success.

Clear out, by an easy imaginative feat, all
the distrusts and timidities, all the fears of
looking ridiculous which you may hardly suspect of being treacherous trouble-makers in
your life. You will find that if you can imaginatively capture the state of mind which
would be yours if you knew you were going
towards a pre-arranged and inevitable success, the first result will be a tremendous surge
of vitality, of freshness. Then—well, the only
way to put it is that it will seem as though
your mind gave a great sigh of relief, of grati-
tude for the liberation, and stretched itself
to its fullest extent. This is the moment where
one may be forgiven for feeling that there is
something truly magical about the whole af-

fair. There will appear an extension of capacity which seems more than normal.

Then the long-dammed-up flow sets in: directly, irresistibly, turned at last in the right direction, the current gathers strength from minute to minute. At first you may still harbor some fear that the spell which worked so instantaneously may break in the same way. It will not, simply because it is no spell; it is a reminder to yourself of the way in which work can always be successfully undertaken. If you remember that, far from your seeing the successful action stop, you will find that each hour of unhampered activity opens out into a promise of others in the future. There may actually be some embarrassment from seeing too many expanding possibilities until you have learned to organize your new life.

Those fears, anxieties and apprehensions, you see, were far more than mere negative things. By acting *as if* they were important, you endowed them with importance, you turned them into realities. They became parasitic growths, existing at the expense of everything that is healthy in you. While we allow them to sap us, we are allowing the nourishment which should go towards expanding growth to be used for feeding monsters, cherishing the freaks and by-blows of the mind instead of its extraordinary and creative elements. So that it is not that one is suddenly given wonderful new powers; by ceasing to let fear hold its frustrating sway *we come into the use of already existing aptitudes which we formerly had no energy to explore.* We discover that we already possess capacities we had not suspected, and the effect, of course, is as though we had just received them. And the rapidity with which these capacities make themselves known when once the aspects are favorable for them is truly somewhat startling. It is even more enjoyable.

Next, there is the further experience of seeming to become, in contrast with one's old self, practically tireless. Actual records of working periods introduced by using this formula would strain the credulity of those who have never yet had the experience. And

these periods are not followed by any depressed reaction. There is always so much
ahead, and it is so clearly seen, that there is no
chance for depression to set in. When the
mind is turned back from its onward drive to
consider all the tribulations of the past, all
the possible mischances which might con-
ceivably happen, it cannot, of course, at the
same time explore the road into the future.
But once absolve it of the thankless and unnecessary task, and it rewards you by seeming
to fly where before it had stumbled and
groped.

It takes some self-education to learn how
to go from one item of successful work to the
next, not to lose time and spend strength—
much more happily, but just as surely—in
gloating over either the ease with which the
task was done or in contemplating too fondly
the truly remarkable work one has just been
so fortunate as to produce. But a few days'
Harvest-Home is quite excusable; and since,
still resilient and unexhausted, one looks
forward to further activity with enjoyment,

there is no permanent danger that the first success under the new régime will be the last.

If you are tempted to look askance at this procedure, to feel that you are being invited to deceive yourself into a feeling of success, you are quite wrong. We are all pragmatists and empiricists in our daily life; what "works" for us is our practical truth, and becomes the basis of our further activity. "Our thoughts become true in proportion as they successfully exert their go-between function," as William James says. And even more fully and convincingly, the late Hans Vaihinger worked out these conceptions in his book, *The Philosophy of "As If."* Not everyone will go with him to the furthest boundaries of his theory, but it is certainly plain that in most matters of life each of us must act "as if" this or that fact were a self-evident truth. For one thing, if we insisted on proving the reality or efficacy or even probability of most of the conceptions on which we base our practical procedures, we should have no time left in which to act. So, in general, we accept the premises for action which are presented to us on good authority, and use them as proved unless or until our experience causes us to doubt the wisdom of so doing. Then we may reëxamine them and perhaps reach different conclusions from our mentors, but for the most part we all act *as if* our norms of conduct, our standards of values, were eternally and everywhere valid, so long as they prove practicable for us.

In everyday life, then, if you are ineffectual in your daily encounters and unproductive in your work, you are to that extent acting *as if* you willed to fail. Turn that attitude inside out, consciously decide that your "As If" shall be healthy and vital, shall be aimed towards accomplishment, and you have made success a truth for yourself.

"The law of nature is: Do the thing and you shall have the power; but they who do not do the thing have not the power."

CHAPTER VI

THE SYSTEM IN OPERATION

IF you are the possessor of a very vivid imagination, you will probably be already well on the way towards practice with no more than the clue in that sentence: Act as if it were impossible to fail. If you are not, or if you have been badly hurt by failure, there may be some difficulty in beginning to act effectively, but there need not be very much.

To get at it more slowly, the idea is just this: instead of starting wherever you are—or, to be accurate, instead of trying to start, or swearing that you *will* start, or deceiving yourself into thinking that you are going to start tomorrow or the day after—beset by all the usual doubts of your own performance and memories of past pain, take time first to "make up" your state of mind, the mental condition in which you are going to work.

If you have an important appointment you do not rush out to it unkempt, unwashed, in any old clothes. You take some trouble to make yourself look as well as you can. Man or woman, you brush and clean your clothes, you look for your good points and emphasize them, you hide or improve your blemishes. Then, when you go to your appointment, you try to act as much as possible as if that heightened condition were your normal state.

Now, you are *mentally* going to an appointment, an appointment with your successful self. How can you arrange your frame of mind to make that appointment fruitful?

You first give yourself a model. Everyone has had a taste of success in some line, perhaps in a very minor matter. Think back to it, however childish it was, even if it was a success of your schooldays. It needn't be, even remotely, success in the adult work you hope to do. What you want to recapture is the *state of mind* in which you once succeeded. Be careful, now; you do not want to overshoot the mark. Don't jump ahead into the elation which followed the success itself. Just recapture the steady, confident feeling that was yours when you knew the fact that was demanded of you, when you realized that you could do the thing that was necessary, that what you were about to do was well within your powers. Try to bring back as clearly as you can every surrounding circumstance of that moment. Now transfer in imagination that success-sequence to the work in hand. If you were absolutely certain that everything about the present work would go as smoothly as everything went when you succeeded in the past, if you knew that what you are beginning would certainly go well, from the moment you begin till the moment of the work's ultimate reception, how would you feel? How would you act? What is the state of mind you would be in as you launch out into it?

Fix your attention on that, for that is to be your working frame of mind. Until you can reach it, refuse to begin; but *insist* to yourself on reaching it as soon as possible. When you have found the mood hold it steadily for a while, as if waiting for a word of command. All at once you will feel a release of energy. You have received from yourself your working-orders, and you can begin. You will see that you no longer have to *push yourself to do the work;* all your energy is free *to push the work alone.*

It was that extra, unnecessary labor of pushing your own inertia aside which made it seem, before, that you were too hampered to get started, were groping through a fog to get at your object, or were stopping continually to brush away half-realized doubts, anxieties, memories of failure that buzzed about you like a cloud of gnats. Clear all that away *before* you begin to work by the simple expedient of refusing to contemplate the mere possibility of failure.

Next, work till you feel the unmistakable onset of true fatigue. *True* fatigue. The early flagging of attention will be only the old state of mind trying to creep in once more when

—89—

your attention is elsewhere. If that happens, stop a second and say to yourself, "No. That is the way I *will not* think!" clear out the impulse entirely, and go on working. When your muscles and your mind honestly protest that they have done all they should do for the time, stop and find some relaxation. If you are held by office-hours, go away quietly alone for awhile when the old state of mind seems in danger of returning, or when you find that you are going to have to spend some time in altering the attitude of a fellow-worker before you can move smoothly in the new way. Stay alone until you have re-established your confident attitude, then return to the group.

When the time for relaxation comes you will find that you get the full joy of playing at last.

There are some persons who have been so badly bruised that, although any unwarrantable indulgence towards oneself should be guarded against, it may be necessary to begin this system by practising it only for a short time each day, and on some secondary desire.

Most educators agree that the best way to teach a child to act confidently and competently, and to facilitate the process of learning, is to ask him first to perform some small task which is well within his untrained powers. As Dorothy Canfield Fisher says in her excellent little book for parents and teachers, *Self-Reliance*, "Success or failure in adult life depends largely on the energy, courage and self-reliance with which one attacks the problem of making his dreams come true. Self-confidence in any enterprise comes as a rule from remembrance of past success." And, again, Professor Hocking in *Human Nature and Its Remaking:* "Education consists in supplying the halted mind with a method of work and *some examples of success.* There are few more beautiful miracles than that which can be wrought by leading a despairing child into a trifling success; and there are few difficulties whose principle cannot be embodied in such simple form that success is at once easy and revealing. And by increasing the difficulty by serial stages, the small will, under the cumulative excitement of repeated and mounting success, may find itself far beyond the obstacle that originally checked it."

So in our own cases, when self-confidence has been lost, should we find some little desire which for some reason has never been gratified. There are scores of these opportunities in every life. All that is necessary, in these experiments toward success, is either that some desire should be taken from the realm of dreaming into that of realization, or that a procedure which was not the perfect one for the effect to be produced should be corrected.

You remember the immortal Bunker Bean, and how his life changed when he was persuaded by the fraudulent medium that he was the reincarnation of a Pharaoh? His rise in the world was rapid; one success followed another and brought a third in its train. When at last he knew he had been cheated, that he was no incarnation of Rameses, nor was the mummy-case that had been sold him made of wood that ever saw ancient Egypt, he had so learned the technique of success that he could not slip back into obscurity. If you observe any family likeness to H. T. Webster's Mr. Milquetoast in yourself, it might be worth your while to get *Bunker Bean* and reread it; the time will not be wasted, since it is only a little less funny than it is fundamentally true.

Here are some examples of developing secondary talents so that confidence in important matters follows:

There is a notably successful physician in New York who recently learned to model in clay, and went on to learn the coloring and glazing of pottery. He did it with the direct intention of giving himself the experience of success in an avocation, since his profession, which is psychiatry, calls on him to deal constantly with refractory material. The confidence which he gains in one line is carried over into his difficult daily work; and in addition he has an engrossing hobby which freshens his mind and has become one more source of approval, since his modelling has come to be always amusing and frequently really distinguished. He must have had a great deal of talent, you may think. Well, what he *did* have was the knowledge that he had always been attracted by the idea of modelling; he had never touched clay until he was in his thirties. He simply took a desire which almost everyone has felt at some time or other and turned it into a source of pleasure and added self-confidence.

Again, in the Art Institute of Chicago there is a room called by the name of a business man who learned to paint after he was fifty. His work, entered in a competition in which his name could not possibly be known, took a first prize. There is now a club of middle-aged business and professional men in Chicago who are studying art and producing good work.

A thirty-year-old clerk in a business office who had had no early advantages had wanted all her life to play the piano. One day on her walk home, moved by an impulse which she fortunately did not resist, she turned into a house which advertised music-lessons by a little sign in the window. Her success, of course, is only comparative. She has not the time needed to make a really excellent musician, nor did she begin early enough to train the special muscles that a professional pianist uses. But she succeeded in reference to her own goal. Her whole life has been altered by that moment of courage. Besides the pleasure she has had from understanding music as only the performer can ever understand it, she has, and knows she has, acted in an adult fashion which resulted in giving her more confidence in every relation of her life. From being the over-worked and oppressed drudge of her home, she came to live in her own small apartment, she visits her family on terms of amicable indifference, and has made a group of friends whose tastes coincide with hers.

These three cases should give a hint, at least, of the proper procedure. Take a definite step to turn a dream into a reality. Say, for instance, that you want to travel and have never been able to do so. When this dream is to be removed from the region of dreams to the region of reality there are several things which must be done. If you are not doing them, you are giving yourself good evidence that you are letting your infantile unconscious dictate the terms of your living rather than your rational mind. If you want to see Italy, for instance, you will certainly enjoy Italy better if you can speak a few words of the language, read a current newspaper in Italian, or know of Italy's past. Do you? Yet there are many excellent small grammars, phrase-books and histories; and how better can you get started than quietly to buy one of these? What else will you need? Time and money. Well, reverse the usual phrase and say to yourself, what is certainly true, that money is time: that if you have a fund of money on which to travel you have also a fund of time. Start in to get it. Put aside a small coin each day, but don't stop there. Think what work you can do in your spare time that will bring you a little more money for your journey. If it is nothing more than to sit with children while their parents are at parties, and if you think of the payment as absolutely dedicated to your intention to travel, you will be acting towards a successful life.

A young and hard-worked assistant editor, wanting to travel, found his way to the offices of an Italian newspaper printed in New York, there received help in translating an advertisement he had written into Italian, in which he offered to exchange lessons in English or in Journalism for lessons in Italian. Two years later he went to Italy as tutor-companion to a young boy, and today he is secretary in a minor capacity in the diplomatic service: the goal he always had in view for himself, but had for years considered unattainable because he had to live up to the very edge of his financial margin.

Be careful that you do not turn these first steps into merely a more elaborate way of playing the old game of day-dreaming with yourself. Do something every day towards your intention, however remote your goal may have to be. If you like to model, stop at a ten-cent store and buy plasticine tomorrow;

if to travel, write for folders; at the very least, if you have no money to spend at all, you can go to, or get into correspondence with, the nearest public library, and learn to use the expert services of librarians.

At first say as little as possible to others of what you intend to do. Get an effect before beginning to talk. If you talk too soon you may almost come to feel that there is a conspiracy against your doing anything out of your usual routine; you will be at least partly right. Those who are still slaves to dreams, to the Will to Fail, are made uncomfortable by the sight of anyone who is breaking free. They feel that there is in the unwonted action some criticism directed at themselves, and become uneasy. At any moment, the Unconscious knows, its supremacy may be disturbed, its opportunities for revery taken away from it. So it begins to fight. One of the most universal forms this combat takes is that of quotation; maxims which sound wise, but which are usually only self-consolatory, spring to the lips of those who reject reality. "The skies change," they will say to you, sententiously; "the heart remains the same," but they will not be quoting in the sense of the original. Or "The grass is always greener on the other side of the fence" you will hear, from those who cannot be bothered to look beyond their own front yards. And so the subtle process of undermining your enthusiasm, and bolstering themselves in their own opinion, will go on. If proverbs fail, they will fall back on teasing.

Now you, if you are at last tearing yourself free, are entering into a conspiracy with Reality, an agreement to see how much may be got out of life if you act with a little more directness and courage than you have used before. Don't put yourself into a position to be discouraged at the start, or bullied out of, or teased about, your new program. Within a short time the results of your action will speak for themselves, providing you with all the justification you need.

Always your first question to yourself should be, "What would I be doing now if it were really impossible for me to fail at—whatever it is: travelling, modelling, writing, farming?" It may be any of these things, or any one of a hundred more: to dance, or dress-make, study calculus or Greek, become better looking, or hear more music. Whatever it is, by thinking, you can discover easily what the first step would be if you were engaged with reality, and not with a dream of a different life. Now you *are* engaged with reality; take that first step. Then ask yourself the next, and so on until you see the ambition itself taking form in your life, beginning to grow with what looks like independent growth, beginning to carry *you* along instead of having to be searched after. For that is what happens: at a certain stage you will find that you are being borne along swiftly and easily on the momentum started by your own initial actions. "Life is infinitely flexible," an old analyst used to say to his patients; and while that may be a little excessive, it is true that life is far more malleable, more flexible, than it seems to be so long as we are unwilling to act.

Or there is another way of starting to act successfully. We seldom realize how great an amount of the friction we all undergo in our lives comes from our expecting to be rebuffed or ignored. Think back to some encounter you had today in your office, in a store, with a servant or tradesman in your home. Try to remember just the form your request took. Making all due allowances for courtesy, or for the respectfulness due to superiors and elders, was there not *in addition* a tentativeness about your request? Didn't you ask for coöperation in such a way as to leave room for refusal, or grudging action, or for being ignored? Now, think of the ideal way in which that question could have been asked, or that order given. It can be cast just as courteously as before, but in such a way that the person of whom you asked help cannot refuse you without being deliberately surly and hostile.

That is the tone of success. When you find it you benefit not only yourself, but the person with whom you must coöperate for effectiveness. Do not waste another's time and energy

or your own patience by suggesting even in-
directly that there is more than one course of
action, if there is *only* one which will get the
result you require. The work to be done takes
half the time if the attention is undivided and
so is free to go on to the next demand quickly.

Have you ever been in an office where, let
us say, a worker who considers herself rather
too well-bred for the position she fills is one
of your co-workers? "Oh, Mr. Robinson," she
will say, elaborately, "if you have just a moment to spare, will you go over those reports
on your desk some time soon? I hate to trouble
such a busy man, but Mr. Smith wants them."
Now, deplorable or not, it is just plain ornery
human nature to wish you *hadn't* just a moment to spare, to cast around you almost automatically for something else you might be
doing which would make you far too busy to
get to that request right away. Yet probably
going over those reports is the next thing on
your program, anyway; if you succumb to the
temptation to hold up the work and teach the
ex-countess a lesson, you hold up the whole

work of the office and get into trouble with your superior officers. Now, wasn't your time and energy wasted by the unfortunate way that simple request was made? Yet the chances are that you yourself say, "Miss Thomas, will you get me the Drummond correspondence, if you aren't too busy?", when it is Miss Thomas' function to get the correspondence at your request whether she is otherwise busy or not; when she will have to say "Certainly," and pretend that she is free to refuse if she likes. It would be just as simple to say "Miss Thomas, I need the Drummond correspond-ence"—which would release her to go straight to the task, feeling that she was not receiving a consideration more than half-patronizing, and not even needing to make a perfunctory reply. If the tone of the simpler sentence is courteous and considerate you have not only left her feelings unwounded, you have treated her as your willing co-worker and given her cause not to think of herself as a touchy sub-ordinate who must be mollified.

These seem such minor matters, but it is

the sum of small things successfully done that lifts a life out of bondage to the humdrum. Women are particularly subject to using the wrong tone to subordinates or office associates, and many of the charges that women are discriminated against in business come from the fact that quite unconsciously they import a mistaken polish into their everyday affairs. Women who complain nightly of incompetence or insolence from maids or children, office-girls who have serial stories to tell of impertinence or "office politics," are, in almost every case, the ones really at fault. By approaching their human contacts with the wrong attitude, by using the wrong tone and the wrong words, they open the way for differences of opinion which never need arise.

By going over your day in imagination before you begin it, thinking of all the contacts you are likely to have and how they can best be handled, listening to your own voice and correcting it till you get the tone which is at once courteous and unanswerable, you can begin acting successfully at any moment. By doing so you will find that you get through your business day with less fatigue; with what you have left you can begin to realize some minor wish of which you have long dreamed in secret. From there it is only a step to finding the courage to begin to do the major things which you have wanted and hoped to do.

CHAPTER VII

WARNINGS AND QUALIFICATIONS

B EFORE going further, it may be well to issue a few statements as to what this system does not include.

The advice *is not* to hypnotize yourself into success. This is important to understand, for many people, and with some reason, dread and fear anything that is based on hypnotism, even in the form of self-suggestion. The work of the Nancy school, with which Coué made us all familiar, is full of excellent hints for self-management, and Charles Baudouin's book, *Suggestion and Autosuggestion,* can be read to great advantage by many who do not follow him with full agreement; and there are several small handbooks on Coué's system which are worth studying. But it is not for nothing that the fad which was once so wide-spread has faded away. In spite of all warnings, too many of those who attempted self-cure ended by reinforcing the troubles they set out to banish.

No, although a sentence from a chapter on hypnotism was helpful in discovering our formula, the connection of this procedure with hypnotism ends there. You are advised to use, first, a minimum of will—just enough to decide to try a new process. Then, as in the Nancy school, the imagination takes over until your mind is clear, cool, and "pleasant" in tone; not confused, diverted, troubled or foggy.

The difference lies just here: in intensive autosuggestion there is a serious danger that the mind will get as out of touch with reality in the other direction as it was in its day-dreaming or depression; that it will become, as the French say, *exaltée*, a word for which we have no exact and satisfactory equivalent. But "extravagantly elated" is about what *exaltée* implies, a state of mental intoxication

—107—

as dangerous as it is temporarily delightful. You cannot live on those peaks; and if you could, you would, again, find yourself unable to act effectively in the world of reality. Without such action you are as far from success, as deep in self-delusion, as ever.

Confident, steady, freely-flowing action is what we need. Then safe delight begins. The mind, cleared of its doubts, begins to expand and enjoy its own activity; the rewards of satisfactory action begin to show themselves. An elation which has nothing to do with delusion or hypnotism naturally follows, and has no later reaction to nullify it.

Second, the advice *is not* to make "affirmations" such as "I cannot fail," "I am successful in all I do," and so on. This procedure, which is helpful with many, has too much in common with auto-hypnotism for those who do not thoroughly understand the principle on which they are working as they follow it. There is much to admire in the philosophy behind those religions which use "affirmations"; that there is an ultimate Unity behind the duality or diversity of the world seems an inescapable conclusion. Nevertheless, we are "conditioned" (as both Behaviorists and philosophers say) by the flesh, by personality, by the concrete world; so we must at least act *as if* the constitution of the world were dual, almost evenly distributed between good and evil. Most of us are brought up short by prosaic commonsense when we try to use the "affirmative" method, and for one who can successfully make use of it there are a hundred who feel ludicrous when doing so. There are others who succeed for a while and then find themselves worse off than before. There is no disapproval whatever for the method when used by those for whom it is, we might say, temperamentally suitable. But for sceptics of even a mild order, it is likely to be more irritating than helpful.

Thirdly, the advice *is not* to dash out and impress others by posing, pretending or downright lying about one's successfulness. The only one to impress, at least at first, is yourself, and that only to the extent of making for yourself a congenial working-atmosphere.

The recommendation, once more, is simply this: *Act as if it were impossible to fail.*

Then, above all, you are not advised to engage in still one more fantasy about success, a somewhat more detailed and circumstantial fantasy than you have pushed yourself to before, but still bearing signs of its kinship to your former day-dreaming. In this case the use of the imagination is quite different, and worth a little detailed scrutiny later.

Long before Freud made his contribution to modern thought, Pico della Mirandola, in a treatise called *De Imaginatione*—Concerning the Imagination—was discriminating between two kinds of revery: the one retrograde, backward-turning, keeping the man from his man's work, prolonging irresponsibility and mental childhood; the other, the true imagination, was found in the successful man.

An aphorism of Joubert, which denies the fine name of Imagination to the former type of revery, is perhaps the neatest definition that can be found, worth pages of ordinary "distinguishing": "Fancy," he says, "an animal faculty, is very different from imagination, which is intellectual. The former is passive, but the latter is active and creative."

It is the latter creative imagination which is to be called on, and if that fact is kept fully in mind there will be no danger of slipping once more into the bad old habit of dreaming the world into a different shape while life slips away. Remember again that "Success depends on a *plus* condition of mind and body, on power of work, on courage." It is that idea which must be held firmly in mind: that the test of whether or not one is dreaming or imagining correctly is whether or not action follows the mental work. Any mental activity which turns backward for longer than it takes to correct a mistake and to replace an unsatisfactory habit with a good one, is *minus,* and cannot be continued if you hope to lead a fuller life.

You set for yourself in advance the hours in which you will work. Within those hours, and as part of that work, you first clear and

WAKE UP AND LIVE!

free your mind. When this has brought you to a pleasant, confident, quiet state you are ready to get at the work proper. The first part of the time is spent clearing the decks for action. You clear the decks; you *act*.

Now, this is an age of alibis. We all know a little too much about the Glands Regulating Personality, and the Havoc raised by Resistances, and so on. Never since the world began were there such good opportunities to be lazy with distinction. It is perfectly true that many cases of subnormal energy can be helped by the proper glandular dosage, but how many of those who have spoken to you of being probably hypo-thyroid * ever went through the simple process of having a basal metabolism test to see if that were really the trouble? Of course they can claim that the situation is so grave that they cannot even get up energy to start being cured; there's no answer to *that* one. But if you are really seriously handi-

---

* It is *hypo,* or sub-thyroid that I mean. Symptom: lethargy. The *hyper*-thyroid is usually overactive. D. B.

capped by lethargy, you can take your first successward step by consulting a good diagnostician, if necessary. If necessary, mind; for there is a fact which makes a good deal of the talk about glandular insufficiency look like the alibi it too often is, and which will be confirmed for you by specialists in glandular therapy if you ask them: that if those who complain of lethargy increase their habitual activity little by little the glands respond by increased secretion. In short, very often this condition can be cured by starting at the other end! You may rest assured that you will have no consequent breakdown in following this advice unless you deliberately (and with intent to cripple yourself) leap from a practically comatose state to one of manic activity.

As for Resistances! They are almost an item of dogma in the current secular religion. Persons who would never dream of going to the time, expense, or trouble of a full analysis will tell you complacently that they have "a resistance" to this or that, and feel that they have done all and more than can be asked of them by admitting their handicap. Remarkable cures of resistances, however, have been observed in those who took solemnly the advice to replace that word with our ancestors' outmoded synonym for the same thing: "bone-laziness." It is not quite so much fun, nor so flattering, to be foolishly lazy as it is to be the victim of a technical term, but many are crippled for knowing an impressive word who would have had no such trouble if they had lived in a simpler and less self-indulgent society. Those who are genuinely, deeply, and unhappily in the grip of a neurosis should turn at once to one of the well known therapies. Unless one is willing to do so, it should be made a matter of social disapproval to refer technically to such difficulties.

If the alibis of the age were in any way generally helpful, if they were not excuses for remaining inactive, and if inactivity were really a happier state than effectiveness, there would be little harm in indulging in the contemporary patter, even without the specialized medical or psychological knowledge nec-

even though we are no longer children. But that again means that we are being provided with advance excuses for failure. If we act on the advice of another and are unsuccessful, obviously the failure is not ours but our counsellor's; isn't that plain? So we can continue to day-dream of successful action, to believe that if only we had followed our first impulse we could not have failed.

Since such motives *can* be present, it is wise to scrutinize every impulse to ask for advice. If the origin of the desire is above suspicion, then there is only one further question to ask before seeking help with a clear conscience: "If I worked this out for myself, would I consume only my own time?" If the answer to that is "Yes," then it is generally better to work out the problem independently, unless the amount of time so expended would be grossly disproportionate to the importance of the result.

If you are a creative worker, remember that time spent in finding an independent technique is seldom wasted. We are accustomed to

think of the success of a man like Joseph Con-
rad, a Pole, in writing the English language,
or of the work of an electrical genius like
Steinmetz, as savoring of the miraculous. To
have had to work out their problems alone—
what a tremendous obstacle to overcome! On
the contrary; the necessity for independent
action was one of the conditions of their success, and to see and admit this is in no way to
detract from the worth of their accomplishment. Most of us support each other and are
in turn supported to such an extent that we
can make almost no individual contribution;
the final result of our labors is a sort of *olla
podrida,* a medley of tastes, talents and tech-
niques, with little to differentiate it from similar results. Look, for a moment, at any of the
run-of-the-mill novels of the day; at the lay-
out, wording and illustration of the adver-
tisements in any given magazine; at the comic
strips in a number of papers. Would it seem
too far-fetched to say that although one man,
one woman, or one firm is actually behind
each of these bids for our attention, they all

seem to have been issued from a sort of central bureau? Yet however uncomplainingly we absorb these issuances from the Ministry for Novel-Writing, the Central Bureau for the Production of Comic Strips, the Committee in Charge of National Advertising, we save our real rewards for those who bring us freshness or genius.

So the working out, however laborious, of an original technique is worth the time expended, the loneliness entailed. With that well in mind, let us consider those times when advice should be taken.

You have a genuine problem. The first step, then, should be to write it out, or to formulate it verbally with exactness, so that you can see just what it is that is troubling you. If you simply let the problem wash around in your mind, it will seem greater, and much vaguer, than it will appear on close examination. *Then* find your expert, whether friend or stranger, but make every effort to find one whose views seem to be congenial to you, since that usually implies similar or congenial mental processes. To do so earlier will mean that you are wasting both your time and his by making him the audience of part of your self-examination. If you are successful in getting an interview, make that as short and concise as possible while still covering all your points. Then follow the advice you are given until you see definite results. If you are tempted to say "Oh, that won't work for me," then you should suspect your own motives. Such a rejection implies that you already had a course of action in mind, and were more than half-hoping that you would be advised to follow it. Watching an example of the wrong attitude towards advice and instruction here may be more illuminating than any positive example.

Have you ever seen the teacher of an art class at work? Frequently he will find in the drawing of one pupil a flaw which is so typical of most students' work at the same stage that he will call the other pupils of the class around the easel. Using the imperfect canvas as his text, he will branch into criticism, advice, exhortation, and will occasionally go on to rub out the mistake and draw the line or put in the color as it should have been done. If you will observe the group at this moment you will discover that, tragically enough, everyone seems to be benefiting by the lecture except the very pupil to whom it should be most valuable. In almost every case the one whose work is providing the example will be quivering, nervous, sometimes tearful, often angry —in short, giving every sign that he is feeling so personally humiliated and insulted that he is reacting at an infantile level. If you ask for help, or put yourself into the relation of a pupil to a teacher, learn to advance by your mistakes instead of suffering through them. Keep your attitude impersonal while you are being shown the road back to the right procedure.

If you are in school, or taking class or private instruction, it is wise to take every opportunity to ask well-considered questions, then to act on the information, and finally— and very important—to report to your instructor as to your success or failure through following his advice. This is of advantage not only to you, but to him and his subsequent pupils, since he cannot know what practices are effective and what are only useful to himself and a few like him unless his pupils report in this fashion. If you must consistently report no progress, then one of two things must be true: that you are not fully understanding him, or that you are not working under the right master.

After your period of apprenticeship is over, try not to weaken yourself or bring about self-doubt to such an extent that you must have help on *minor* points of procedure. Every physician and psychiatrist knows that there is a great class of "sufferers" who return again and again, asking so many and such trivial questions that it seems unlikely they could ever have grown to maturity if they were as helpless in all relations as they show themselves to their physicians. No one except a charlatan truly welcomes the appearance of such patients as these. The person who is looking for an excuse to blame his failure on another or who will not, if he can help it, grow up and settle his own difficulties, will go on asking advice until he draws his last breath, and even the astutest consultant may be forgiven if he sometimes mistakes an infrequent questioner for one of the weaker type.

A good touchstone to show whether you may be only following a nervous habit of dependence is to ask yourself in every case: "Would I ask this if I had to pay a specialist's fee for the answer?" All busy persons whose work brings them into the lime-light have frequent requests for personal interviews. Usually they answer as well as they are able, taking much trouble rather than run the risk of rebuffing any talented or sensitive beginner; but they are ruthlessly exploited. When, as sometimes happens, an eminent man comes to the place where he answers no questions of this sort, it is not that he is swollen with conceit, not that he would not gladly help anyone in genuine perplexity, but that he has no certain way of winnowing the sincere inquirers from the neurotics, and, since he still has his

own valuable work to do, he reluctantly decides for silence. To console himself he knows
that many who are ready to do their own work
only frustrate themselves by acting with too
much humility, and that if their questions go
unanswered they will find their own satisfactory solutions.

So talking, complaining, asking advice, inviting suggestions—all are better abandoned
during the period of reëducation. Ultimately
and ideally, of course, you want to be able to
work under any and all circumstances. You
cannot ever be certain that your favorite con-
fidante or your most stimulating friend will
always be in a position to lend a sympathetic
ear at the moment that you feel you need it.
If you establish the habit of going to someone
at a certain point in your work, and lead yourself to feel, even unconsciously, that this is
necessary to a satisfactory performance, you
are laying the foundation of future failure.

Moreover, whatever your field may be, if
you spend every possible moment at creative
activity, you will come to the place where you

have a body of your own work, a total of experience, to consider; you will get the "feeling of your material." Then you will see how
many of your problems arose because you had
previously been in the position of an amateur
or novice, because you had so little experience
in your own line that for a while every problem seemed unique.

CHAPTER IX

THE TASK OF THE IMAGINATION

ALREADY imagination's contribution to a productive life has been considered somewhat, and its help has been called on in the matter of making that favorable mental climate which is necessary if we are to produce our best work. But imagination has innumerable other uses, it can be helpful in ways so diverse that the same faculty hardly seems to be in operation in all of them.

In everyday life, we tend to think of the imagination as something which may, perhaps, be spoken of as "useful" to artists of all sorts, but as being almost the opposite of useful in the lives of practical men and women. To use one's imagination, generally, is thought of as taking a holiday, as allowing the wits to go wool-gathering, the mind to relax and sun itself. After indulging it—for we commonly think of the exercise of the imagination as being in some way an indulgence—we may return refreshed to the commonplace, or we may find we have lost time, missed contacts, got out of step with our companions and helpers: in short, suffered for allowing one part of the mind free play.

As a consequence we look warily at the imagination, often seeking to check it, or, in some extreme cases, even to eradicate it. That it can be of immense benefit in the most prosaic affairs is an idea at which many readers will balk. But that is because they do think of the imagination as a faculty which always wanders unchecked, which must be permitted to make its own rules and occasions, which is incapable of being directed, and, to a great extent, controlled—put at the service of the reason and the will. Thus controlled and directed, it becomes the mature creative imagination, the spiritual faculty of which Joubert speaks.

But consider a few of the many things which it can usefully do for us: it can help us to stand away from ourselves somewhat, holding the emotions and prejudices which often keep us from seeing clearly well in hand. By so doing we may find that we are thwarting our own best interests constantly, and can replace the disadvantageous activities—still in the imagination—by others which will bring about happier results. It can be turned on the character of an opponent or an uncoöperative "helper" while we study him as an author might study a character whom he hopes to place in a book. We can get clues to his motives, and thereafter watch to see whether we have been right about them, thus saving ourselves from such mistakes as being too brusque with a sensitive person, or too laxly indulgent with another who will exploit us if we give him the opportunity.

Nor does this begin to exhaust the ways in which imagination, instead of betraying us into revery and resignation to unsatisfactory conditions—instead, even, of being employed merely as a means of recreation—can contribute to the making of a good life. Working as far as possible under orders from the will, and hand-in-hand with reason, it can explore new fields for our efforts, can bring back to us some of our original freshness towards our work which we have lost by fatigue and routine; it can even perform such a severely practical function for us as to discover new markets for our wares, or new ways in which to use old talents.

These ideas are worth a little closer examination here, and later the insertion of some exercises in using the imagination.

We need not belong to that group which, as we say, "can only learn by experience." Having discovered that much of our dread of engaging in new activity comes from unconquered fear of the pain which we formerly met when we began to go forward, we can decide that some of our "trial-and-error" attempts at managing life shall go on in the mind, in the imagination, where it is, to all intents, painless. We can learn to look ahead imaginatively, and so save ourselves from blunders, ineffectuality, loss of energy and time.

First of all, we can use imagination to see ourselves and our work in some perspective.

Everyone knows how a child identifies himself utterly with all he owns and does, with all those who care for him. He is outraged if asked to share his possessions, the breaking of a beloved toy is a tragedy, if it rains on the day when a picnic was planned one would think the sun could never shine for him again. If a mother or nurse leaves him while he is awake, he has been most treacherously betrayed. In fact, much early education has as its one goal the teaching of the little egotist to see himself in somewhat truer relation to his world. More or less successfully, each of us has had to learn this lesson; but it is almost never fully understood. To our last days there is still a trace of that childish egotism in us—sometimes so very much more than a trace that an adult suffers, resents, sulks, and complains in a way only too reminiscent of the nursery.

There is no success which does not entail a

relationship between the individual and others. (That artist who "works only to please himself" is a chimera, as mythical a beast as the hippogriff.) Since that is so, there will be occasions on which it is immensely important for us to see ourselves clearly, and in scale with those around us. Each of us at some time is in a position to have to say to himself "Here am I; here is the work I do; here are those I hope to help and please by this work." Imagination can help us to stand back and see that relationship in perspective, can analyze its parts and suggest to us the full scope of what we have undertaken.

The infantile adult can never see himself at one remove; even less can he see his work or the object he has made quite as it is, undistorted by the over-estimation of personal pride, or the under-estimation of humility and fear. Consequently he is never in a position to know just where his contribution *does* go in the scheme of his world, and is at the mercy of the reports of friends or strangers. Even here he is bewildered; however plain the words

may be, however just the estimate which is
given him, he will not hear exactly what is said
because he cannot bring to the moment his
undivided and unemotional attention. His
intense preoccupation with his own hopes
and desires spoils him as a recording instru-
ment. He cannot benefit by good advice or
sound criticism; nor, on the other hand, can
he know when such advice is mistaken, and
the criticism not expert. By looking, in imagination, first at himself, then at the work he
wants to do, then at the audience to whom he
hopes to appeal; and, finally, by bringing all
these elements into relation with each other,
he could keep his courage from being under-
mined, his mind unconfused by conflicting
advice, his estimate of his performance just.

Now, to identify ourselves too long with
work we do is a bad mistake, and a mistake
through which we can be hurt and hampered.
The past few years have taught us much about
the folly of so identifying ourselves with our
children that they are rendered incapable of
leading independent lives. The mother who

clings to her adult (or even adolescent) child, suffering with him, making his decisions, undergoing humiliation on his account, unable to live her own life fully if he is not leading the sort of life she covets for him, meddling with his affairs, dictating his professional and social interests, is no longer looked upon as the sum of maternal love and wisdom. While we may not always practise as wisely as we should, few men and women today consider the complete identification of themselves with their children as either praiseworthy or desirable. We have to that extent learned perspective about one of the most fundamental relations of life. We know that our work as parents is to do all in our power to equip the child to live a happy, healthy adult life, to put up no unnecessary barriers before his independent activities, to leave him free to select his friends and to form his own judgments as soon as possible. What is more, we know that it is desirable that every adult, whether parent or child, should have his own interests, and that only the possession of such interests will guarantee that no unwholesome interference with the life of another will take place. Further, no one believes for a moment that because a saner understanding of a parent's functions is replacing the old dictatorship, which was tyrannical even when it was motivated by deep affection, the love between mother or father and child is in any way decreasing.

The analogy of any finished piece of work with a child is very close: each has to be carried, cherished, nourished as part of one's very self during the early stages. But with full growth there comes a time when each should have its independent identity. If we intend to get all we can from living, we must learn when to go on from one task to the next. Even the most productive of us could contribute more than he does; our output is about halved because we do not learn to separate ourselves from the things that are done and put our energy into the work which is ahead. Instead we turn and watch the fortunes of what we have lately been engrossed in. To some extent this is inevitable; we need to know the history and fortunes of our finished work in so far as we can learn anything valuable from them. But here is a place where the average man can learn from the genius. Abundance, as Edith Wharton has said, is the sign of the true vocation; and that is so in any branch of life. Your true genius—whether a Leonardo, a Dickens, a Napoleon, an Edison—is always going on. Versatility and abundance are not, as we are sometimes told, the signs of the mediocre workman. When they are present in a mediocre man, they are, on the contrary, the very things he has in common with the great men of his profession.

So accustomed are we to doing a piece of work, and then standing still to contemplate what happens to it, that we constantly wonder at those who do not make the same error. We even, erroneously, believe that they must "drive themselves" relentlessly in order to accomplish what they manage to do. Now, nothing of the sort is true—or it is not necessarily true. What has happened is that the time, the energy, the attention which in lesser men goes into waiting for approval, listening to comments, wondering whether some item or other might have been better done, is going *forward* and opening up new paths. It is not at all that the healthfully prolific men and women are complacent, or oblivious to real criticism; they know that if anything pertinent is said they will hear it. Experience has taught them that we are never deaf to what truly concerns us. What they have learned is not to *wait* to hear comment; and so their lives are twice as full and satisfactory as those of us who cannot learn when to let the results of our thought and labour, our mental offspring, go out to lead their own lives.

Imagination can bring us to understand how such sane workers operate, and suggest ways in which we can imitate them.

CHAPTER X

ON CODES AND STANDARDS

Bᴜᴛ what if you must have approval and ac-
quiescence in one phase of your work before you go on to the next? What if your work
is contributory to a group-effort? That is, of
course, more complicated, but imagination
can still come to your aid. It can show you
where you stand in the chain of causes which
go to bring about a certain result, and thus
teach you to be patient during the time when
your work is being considered, to hold yourself
in a state of balance until the verdict is passed.
Then, if it is adverse—as it occasionally must
be—you can do one of two things: tackle the
same problem from a new angle, hoping this
time to reach a good working-basis with your
co-workers, or you must put your reasons for

believing that your original idea is good in such a way as to show that you are not defending it simply out of a sense of outraged proprietorship.

The only way to do this successfully is to have a well-thought-out set of standards drawn up for each type of work that you do, and *in advance*. If you wait till any one item is finished you may find yourself reasoning after the fact, defending the fact-accomplished, and perhaps blinding yourself to real insufficiencies in it.

Here again we call on imagination. If you were to envisage the best possible example of the work you are about to undertake, what would it be? Find the best example of similar work that you can. What qualifications does it have? Which ones are vitally necessary? Which were added by the originator of that example? With this analysis in hand, draw up a set of standards for your own use, putting down first those things which are absolutely necessary if you are to succeed at all; next those which are desirable if it is possible to include them; last, but most important to your *personal* success, those things which are your own contribution.

Now, before getting to work, drop your own point of view and see your prospective task from the position of your audience, of the "ultimate consumer." Who is to benefit by the activity? Who, if you are a creative worker, is your audience? Who, if you are selling an article, is your predestined customer? If you were in his shoes, what would you like to see included in the offering? If you can imaginatively enter into the state of mind of those through whom you hope to attain your success, you can frequently add just those elements which will make your work irresistible.

(Take, a very prosaic instance with which we are all familiar, the simple matter of kitchen equipment. Why do you suppose that for years most stoves, sinks, laundry-tubs, continued to be made so low that the women who worked at them tired quickly from the abnormal positions they were forced to take? There was no good reason; but the moment some inspired person thought not merely how all such things were already being made, not merely of selling an adequate object, but of the comfort of those who were to use his product when sold, a revolution in kitchen-equipment came about. Often such an improvement is staring us in the face; an obvious small change can be made which will bring an article, which we all buy in its unsatisfactory form simply because no better one is offered, out of its traditional shape into a form which will have, besides the element of novelty, that of greater convenience or usefulness. That change will only be made by the person who is imaginative about his work, who can not only analyze the present form of an object into its essential parts, but who can imaginatively enter the life of the person who is to use it later.)

Oddly enough, it is more often the creative worker who fails to expand the standards for his work by considering the half-formulated desires of his audience. Part of his intention, at least, must be to convey an idea or an aesthetic emotion to others, and he fails if he does not do so. It is true that to have a constant gnawing fear that you are not pleasing others has a bad effect on work. It is true that if you look *exclusively* to please others what you do will seldom be worth doing; but if your idea of success includes recognition, then the more you can learn imaginatively of your audience the better. If, knowing their tastes, you can give them not only what they want but something much better than they, being non-professionals, could imagine, you are sure of your success.

Having taken all these things into consideration, having formulated as clearly as possible the ideal towards which your own work should tend, before launching it into the world you should check it against a set of questions which arise logically from the possession of well-defined standards. Each line of activity will have a different set, each individual worker will alter the emphasis, or have his own idea of the proper order for these critical questions, but roughly the finished work should be measured in somewhat this way:

Is what I have done as good as the best in its field?

Has it everything necessary for all ordinary purposes?

Have I added any special values by way of an original contribution?

Have I made it as attractive and convenient as possible for those who are its logical users? (Or audience, or clients.)

Have I considered whether there is another group to which it might also be made to appeal?

What more can I do before I release it from myself and send it out to make its own way?

(Try reading these questions in two ways: as referring to an item of commerce; *as an attitude towards a daily task*.)

The artist will necessarily have a different set of questions, although they will be cognate with those above. As an example, one of our best poets asks herself these questions:

Have I conveyed what I thought?

Have I conveyed what I felt?

Is it as clear as I can make it?

Is it as distinguished or beautiful as its matter permits?

Again, if you are one of a group of workers, imagination can help you in still another way, by showing you where you stand in relation to those around you. When you have seen this you can work out a code for yourself which will remove many of the irritations and dissatisfactions of your daily work. Have you ever been amused and enlightened by seeing a familiar room from the top of a stepladder; or, in mirrors set at angles to each other, seen yourself as objectively for a second or two as anyone else in the room? It is that effect you should try for in imagination. If you can see yourself and your fellow workers as impersonally as men on a chess-board, you can often find what it is that you are not doing, or what you are doing imperfectly, and move to correct the bad practice.

Many of those who believe themselves overworked are doing less than they should ideally do, and could do easily if they saw what is expected of them with imagination instead of anxiety. Often the excess work is something which they have almost officiously undertaken, many times from a real sense of duty and obligation. No large office is without one example of this type who is its *reductio ad absurdum,* the panicky job-grabber: from fear lest he, or, usually, she might possibly be considered as not doing all that is expected, or might be considered unnecessary to the organization, he gets a hundred small details in his hands, with the result that he *is* overworked, performance is not perfect, time is lost, and others who might be well occupied have time to idle and lose interest. If such a worker could see his position in perspective he could do more of the work he was really engaged for, do it better, and do it with less sense of strain and fatigue.

Those executives and administrators who continually do far more than they can without incurring fatigue and irritability are frequently pandering to their own self-importance and conceit, although usually they would reject the charge with wrath. They are certainly allowing the Will to Fail to operate in their lives. It is good to extend one's normal activity till its capacity is reached—and that is far oftener much more than we habitually do rather than less—but the tasks taken on thereafter are the first steps towards failure—towards that trouble, beloved of Americans, the "nervous breakdown."

When you have found your function, perform it very fully, but do not overstep it except in emergencies. In most large enterprises, or joint enterprises, there is—or should be—some one person whose decisions are final. Sometimes each member of a partnership has the power of command or veto for one aspect of the work. Often these decisions are given after the opinions of all have been canvassed, or suggestions invited. Right here comes the necessity for a code: *if the decision goes against you or your suggestion, abandon your own idea and coöperate in the decision whole-heartedly*. If you feel that a truly grave mistake is being made, take a few hours to draw up the situation as you see it, show how you think the new decision will alter matters, why you think it is a mistake, or why an alternative plan should be adopted. Try to be as fair about this as you can. Often we think an alternative plan precious because, and only because, it is our own. "Pride of authorship" comes in.

Many of those who believe they *have* given up their own ideas and are working along other lines will unconsciously go on obstructing and objecting, holding up the work, trying to defeat its ends. The trouble here is that this obstructionism *is* often unconscious; but the way to escape the danger is to realize it as a possibility, and to look at yourself and your attitude scrupulously to be sure you are not putting up unnecessary hazards, doing your share of the new program slowly or indifferently—trying to bring about a failure, since your plan was ignored or modified.

If, on the other hand, you are the one whose decisions must be accepted, you will save yourself trouble later by watching the initial stages of the work to be sure that some such unconscious sabotage is not going on. A quick challenge to the troublesome person whose feelings have been hurt will sometimes whip a whole program into shape which might otherwise fail. And by such watching you can see that each is doing the work assigned to him.

A little imaginative overseeing of a staff or partnership in the early stages of any activity will often result in clearing up a disorder of long standing.

Perhaps, however, you are really miscast, and your usefulness would be on, say, the planning end of an enterprise rather than the executive, where you are placed. In that case, your problem is to bring your talents to the attention of your superior officers with as little crowding and bustling as possible. Learn to write clear, short, definite memoranda and present them to your immediate superior until you are perfectly certain that he will never act upon them. In no other circumstances are you justified in going over his head. Try also to be willing to see your work and suggestions acted upon without receiving immediate acknowledgment that the ideas originated with you. This frequently happens in a large organization, and to sulk or stand out for having your rights recognized in every case will only cancel the advance you might have been able to make. If your good idea is one of a series and not a flash in the pan, you can be sure your calibre will eventually make itself felt. If not, the organization is a bad one for you, and you should set about finding a better connection as soon as possible.

Partnerships, and particularly the universal partnership of husband and wife, are almost always individual cases. In general the rule should be, try never to assume what is the *normal* function of the other partner until you have almost indisputable evidence that if you do not do so some vital balance will be destroyed. Often to do one's own part fully and well is enough to call out the complementary activities of the other. In any partnership, once you are sure that you are doing your own part, if there is still some obvious weakness to correct it can usually be talked over, the reason for it found, and its correction arranged. Occasionally this cannot be done. Only those who are in such a relation know when it is impossible to talk over any matter because of an over-sensitiveness or blindness in the other partner. In such cases, assume as much of the overlooked responsibility as you can discharge well, but no more. There is always the possibility of sudden illumination, of belated growth, which will be endangered if you take upon yourself more than you should. But notice that where you must do work not your own, *assume* these responsibilities; see that you do not allow them to be thrust upon you. What you undertake open-eyed will seldom be made later a cause of martyrdom and sullenness.

When once you have seen imaginatively what your scope should be, both as an individual and as a member of a group, a society, or a partnership you are ready to teach, discipline and exercise yourself till you reach your state of maximum effectiveness.

CHAPTER XI

TWELVE DISCIPLINES

I

THERE are dozens of small ways by which we can make our minds both keener and more flexible—two qualities peculiarly necessary for those who intend to live successfully. We all succumb too easily to the temptation to find a routine which works out so that we get our day's tasks done with a minimum of effort and conscious attention; a fact which might have no unfortunate effects on us at all if we used the time we save by our routines to good purpose. But the cold truth is that we do nothing of the sort. We apply the routine-observing tendency to our whole lives, growing mentally and spiritually more flaccid, more timorous, less experimental with every day we spend supported by the rigidity of habit.

Habit takes care of most of our ordinary

activities; we get through our work by using only that part of our intellect which has been trained to consider the work's specific problems (often trained painfully and protestingly); when we meet a novel thought or situation, we fall back on an analogy and act according to the prejudice or emotion which that arouses in us. Even those of us who rather solemnly undertake programs of self-improvement seldom use more than one set of mental muscles, gathering a number of facts about this subject or that, and considering ourselves "improved" if we learn something about the religions of India, or the works of Charles Dickens, or the birds of Southern California.

This would be harmless enough if it were not for the complacency which attends it. Fact-gathering *is* one activity of the intellect; and where a little training in independent judgment has accompanied or preceded it, so that correct conclusions concerning the facts are independently reached, it is a valuable one. But such programs alone do not exercise the mind to its fullest extent, to make an instantaneously useful tool of it, or give one the power to call on all its resources at will.

Even those who think of themselves as extraordinarily hard workers are not in the state of mental training, usually, which allows them to get the most from their lives. One great reason is pointed out over and over by Dr. Alexis Carrel in his book *Man, the Unknown:* the benefits of civilization are not unmixed blessings. We are no longer called on to meet the extremes of heat and cold, for instance, to go through alternate periods of plenty and scarcity of food; universal lighting turns night into day everywhere, and the newspapers and radio entertain us so that we seldom look to ourselves for our own resources. Healthy man has a great capacity for adaptation, and, says Dr. Carrel, "the exercise of the adaptive functions appears to be indispensable to the optimum development of man." We have allowed ourselves to soften, to abandon our ingenuity, to escape responsibility whenever possible, till we grow to fear and abhor the very word "discipline."

Yet discipline is undergoing restraint in order to develop the qualities necessary for a full life. Mental discipline should connote the equivalent in the sphere of the mind which the athlete undertakes for perfecting his body. We should first take stock of our minds; and then set to work on them to strengthen them here, make them more flexible there, stretch them somewhat, teach them to be more exact —in short, put them through their paces so that we get the maximum use and advantage from them.

In order to do so, we must learn to be arbitrary with ourselves—by no means an easy matter for a generation which has not only been softened by material conveniences, but has been given the dubious benefit of being allowed to "psychologize" about itself day in and day out. Some of us dread and dislike restraint, even when self-imposed for a sound purpose, to such an extent that we live our lives between habit and impulse under the impression that only so can we be wholly free. But "Freedom," says Aristotle, "is obedience to self-formulated rules," and the definition holds as good today as two thousand years ago.

We must work to get back tone and muscle into our lives until it is possible to stop one activity and turn to another, varying the approach, stroke, strength behind the effort, and so on, with as much agility and deftness as a skillful tennis-player uses to meet the shifting play of a good opponent. If we could know each day just the necessities we should be called on to meet, we could prepare ourselves in advance, and flexibility and ingenuity would be uncalled for. Since that does not happen, we must get ourselves into training to meet the infinite calls on us, instead of, as we usually do, discharging easily only one or two matters which are natively congenial to us, and getting through the others awkwardly, blindly.

The disciplines suggested here are drawn from all over the world. Readers of philosophy and religion will find procedures they have met before, recommended by the wise men of many countries: there are disciplines from India and Spain, from Greece and China—and from any girl's finishing school! Some of them are common to every country which teaches any kind of mental or spiritual discipline, such as that of observing set periods of silence. None of them is "arbitrary" in the sense of "pointless"; each develops or strengthens a faculty of the mind which should be kept in good condition if a life is to be led purposefully and under one's own control.

Not all of them will be equally valuable to all cases; but before rejecting any one of them examine yourself to discover if you are not possibly throwing it aside simply because it *does* ask you to put a little more restraint on yourself than you find pleasurable. Most of them will be difficult at some stage, attended by something in the mental realm like the stiffness and soreness which follow using a new muscle in athletic training. But you can exercise muscle only by submitting it to some sort of resistance; you must feel at least slightly uncomfortable to have the assurance that your exercise is doing the work you are asking of it. So, in following these mental exercises, unless there is some discomfort from observing each one fully, unless there is some protest arising from interrupted habits and novel ways of action, it may be that the discipline in question is not one that you really need. Replace it, in that case, with another which calls on you for some endurance and effort.

II

THE TWELVE DISCIPLINES

1.

The first exercise is to spend an hour every day without saying anything except in answer to direct questions. This should be done in the midst of your usual group, and without giving anyone the impression that you are sulking or suffering from a bad headache. Present as ordinary an appearance as possible; simply do not speak. Answer questions just to their limit, and no further; give a full and adequate answer, but do not continue with volunteered remarks which are suggested by the answer or question, and do not attempt in any way to draw another question from your interlocutor. Oddly enough, this is a difficult discipline for even a normally taciturn person. We are all so used to breaking into speech whenever we meet one another, merely in order to give evidence of our friendliness and accessibility, that we talk almost constantly whenever there is an opportunity.

This discipline is found in almost every country which is the home of a genuinely old religion. It is of immense value, and productive of many different results. Probably no two experimenters ever have identical reactions to this practice; they will vary according to temperaments. One thing which soon becomes apparent to many, for instance, is that we seldom say exactly what we mean at our first attempt. We rush into speech, see by the expression on another's face that we have not made ourselves entirely clear, or have misspoken in some way, and try again. This likewise may not make our intention understood; we try again. We pause a moment, think the matter over, issue a clearer statement. But in the meanwhile there are those three earlier attempts to express ourselves still remaining in our hearers' minds, beclouding the issue.

One man, reporting on this experiment, said that he seemed at first not to be there at all. Then there was a period when he felt that he, in his silence, filled the whole room and had the experience of seeing it all impersonally. As long as he talked, wherever he stood was, naturally, the center of his scene; silent, the group "composed" with a different emphasis. When his hour was over he saw himself sometimes in the center, sometimes on the circumference, occasionally entirely outside the interests around him.

Another man recorded that when his silence began to make itself felt the friends he was with acted most illuminatingly. Not quite aware what made the occasion unusual, two of them were definitely ill at ease. One thereupon became extremely ingratiating, a second truculent and then downright hostile, arriving at the point of charging his silent friend with feeling "superior" just as the hour was up and speech could be resumed. A third man, heretofore the quietest of the group of friends, turned extremely talkative, as though to retrieve a balance he felt endangered, relapsing into silence when the observer began to talk naturally again.

A woman reported, with much amusement, that she had never had such a personal success in her life as during the hour she sat silent and smiling at a party. Her silence seemed to act as a magnet and a challenge in a way her gaiety had never done.

All experimenters, however, agreed on one matter: while the silence lasted a sense of mastery grew in them. When they resumed speech it was with the sense of using speech definitely and purposefully, and always with the knowledge that the resort of silence could be found at will. One concluded her report with a sentence from Meredith which she said she had never fully understood before: "It is the silence of the god we fear, not his wrath; Silence is the unbearable repartee."

2.

Learn to think for half-an-hour a day *ex-clusively on one subject*. Simple as this sounds, it is at first ludicrously hard to do. The novice should begin by thinking on his solitary subject for five minutes a day at first, increasing the period daily till the half hour has been attained. To begin with, a concrete object should be chosen: a flower, a bottle of ink, a scarf. Do not have it before you; build it up in your mind. With a flower, for instance, describe it to yourself as each of the senses would report it. When that is done, go on to how it grows and where; what it symbolizes, if anything; what uses are made of it. From this simple beginning, work up to considering a concrete problem, and, finally, to an abstraction. Start with subjects which really interest you, but when you have taught your mind not to wander even for a moment, begin choosing a subject by putting your finger at random on a newspaper or the page of a book, and think on the first idea suggested by the lines you have touched.

You will find it very revealing to start this exercise with a pencil and pad, and to make a slight check on the paper whenever you find your attention slipping. If you are really quick to realize when your mind has begun to wander, you will find your paper very full for the first few days. Fortunately, improvement in this is fairly rapid. At the end of a week in some cases, at the end of a month even in refractory ones, the pad will be found nearly blank at the end of your half-hour. The value of this exercise must be obvious to anyone who hopes to engage in original work, or to introduce new procedures of any sort. At first it is wise to practise this when alone; but eventually you should be able to do it even in the midst of distractions, such as when travelling to and from work.

(Note carefully that the recommendation is not to hold one's mind immobile on one object, as in some Indian disciplines or in the Christian process called "recollection." You are to think about one subject only; no more than that. The other practice induces a slightly

hypnoidal state, and is not suitable to our purposes here.)

This, of course, is simply the "application"
and "concentration" which was preached to
every one of us in our school days. It is very
revealing, none the less, to see how imperfectly
we learned that lesson then or at any subsequent time! Once it is learned, it is of immense benefit. Anyone who is capable of it,
for instance, can pick up a foreign language in
very short order. The accent may be bar-
barous, unless one has learned phonetics
early, but books and newspapers can be
easily read, and enough of a vocabulary to get
around in the strange land can be acquired in
less than a month.

Moreover, in any competitive performance,
the one who has trained himself to think
steadily, without deflection, will arrive at his
conclusions first. But the advantages of this
are too obvious to need emphasizing further.

3.

Write a letter without once using the fol-

lowing words: I, me, my, mine.* Make it
smooth and keep it interesting. If the recipient
of the letter notices that there is something
odd about it, the exercise has failed.

This practice, and others like it, again allows us to see ourselves in perspective. In
order to write a good letter of the sort, it is
necessary to turn the mind outward, to give
up for a while the preoccupations and obses-
sions with our own affairs. We come back to
our own lives refreshed.

4.

Talk for fifteen minutes a day without using I, me, my, mine.

5.

Write a letter in a "successful" or placid
tone. No actual misstatements are allowed. No
posing as successful, no lying. Simply look for
aspects or activities which *can* be honestly reported in this way and confine your letter to

---

* In my innocence, I believed this exercise was
wholly mine. I recently came across it, and similar
exercises, in Alys Bentley's *The Dance of the Mind*.

them. Indicate by the letter's tone that you are, at the moment of writing, not discouraged in any way.

There is a double purpose here. First, it is a simple way of turning from a negative and discouraging attitude towards a positive and healthy one. However unpromising the prospect for finding enough good items for a letter may appear at first, one soon discovers that a number of matters are going smoothly and well, but that they have been ignored while one centers on disappointment and frustration. Second, and more important, such a letter as this, sent to almost every correspondent you have, will remove one great stumbling-block to the successful conduct of your affairs.

Letter-writing is a task we usually tuck into an odd corner of our day. When we have nothing to do and feel listless, bored, tired or depressed, we take pen in hand and write to our dear ones! We send low-spirited, unhappy notes about, and reap the natural consequences: consolatory or sympathetic letters come in answer. Sometimes they come when we are feeling fairly well, or in really high spirits; but it is a heroic character who can resist the chance to feel sorry for himself. We have the choice, reading these answers which we have invited, of slipping back into the mood of martyrdom and self-pity, or of feeling distinctly silly. It is far more dramatic to feel sad again than to feel silly; so we go on in our vicious circle, and send the latest bad news when we write again. A complete holiday from self-pity and depression is necessary to success.

6.

And this exercise comes directly from all the finishing-schools for young ladies that ever existed: pause on the threshold of any crowded room you are to enter, and consider for a moment your relation to those who are in it. Many a retiring and quiet woman can thank this small item of her school training for her ability to handle competently situations which seem as though they would be embarrassing and exacting for anyone so sheltered. It was for years (and may be still, for all I know) the custom to teach young girls to stop just a moment at the door of the room they were entering until they had found their hostess, and then the guest of honor. (Failing such guest, the oldest person in the room was to be singled out.) Then the room was entered, the young guest going, as soon as her hostess was free, straight to her to be welcomed and to "make her manners." She then watched for the first opportunity to speak for a few minutes to the guest of honor; and not until she had discharged these obligations was she free to follow any other plans or inclinations of her own. The girl who thoroughly learned this lesson learned something which is invaluable to everyone: to size up a roomful of people at a glance, discover what it holds, first in the way of obligation and then in the way of companionship or one's own interests.

There is a kind of nonsensical notion abroad today that to take such conscious forethought about any occasion is to be a hypocrite or a snob, that there is some virtue in rushing pell-mell into any situation, snatching what offers itself without difficulty, and foregoing the rest. There is no danger that you will really be acting "artificially" if you give yourself a moment to foresee the various possibilities and relationships in the occasion you are about to live through. You will simply have taken care not to be stampeded into doing something uncongenial to you, of getting caught in a backwater of conversation which touches none of your real interests, or of running the risk of missing a chance to talk to a real friend, or someone whose conversation will bring you something of value. However consciously we plan our lives, there is still enough margin of the unforeseen and the unexpected to keep us from any danger of losing spontaneity, but the *ideal* is to have as much of our lives within our voluntary control as possible. Sometimes, with the best of intentions, we are not able to bring about what we want in that moment of anticipation; if we have taken the trouble to see all the possibilities before us, we can turn to a secondary interest easily, not missing every opportunity because we were disappointed in one.

7.

When the above exercise is learned or re-captured, go on to an old piece of advice from seventeenth-century France: keep a new acquaintance talking about himself or herself without allowing him to become conscious of what you are doing. Turn back, at first, any courteous reciprocal questions in such a way that your auditor does not feel rebuffed. You will find a genuine interest rising in you for your companion; soon, if you are at all kindly or imaginative, you will find yourself engrossed. The last, lingering trace of self-consciousness will drop from you. It may be that you will not be asked about yourself. That makes no difference; at the very least you have learned a little more about how the world looks to another, and have extended your horizon. If, on the other hand, you *do* talk of yourself in response to later questions, you will know just how much to say, what interests you have in common, whether you could ever find the friendship of that person desirable.

(Perhaps it needs to be said plainly that acting consciously need not mean acting coldly. Not a grain of real humanity is sacrificed by having the reins of action in one's own hands; rather the contrary. An outgoing effort is voluntarily undertaken and carried on; instead of being so totally engrossed in ourselves that we know nothing of the moods or interests of others except as they affect us, we escape by the pleasantest road from our restricting egotism. The other party to the experiment, far from being a victim of cold-blooded planning, is for once assured of *not* being victimized by our blind selfishness.)

8.

The exact opposite of the above exercises, and infinitely harder to do with intention: Talk exclusively about yourself and your interests without complaining, boasting or (if possible) boring your companion. Make yourself and your activities as interesting as you can to the person to whom you are talking.

This is an excellent discipline for those who ordinarily talk too much about themselves. This *reductio ad absurdum* of their weakness brings them face to face with the ordeal which they are putting their friends through on every opportunity. When concentrated talking about one's own interests is undertaken consciously, every sign of indifference, of boredom, of restiveness or impatience, of desire to introduce another topic of conversation which may escape us while we are neurotically self-absorbed, is only too plainly seen. Both the exercise and the weakness will be abandoned gratefully after one or two occasions.

However, there are other things to be gained from this. It soon becomes apparent that talking about the trivial, the commonplace, the recurring incidents of one's life leads to certain ennui in our hearers. If, on the other hand, we have had genuinely interesting experiences, have been more imaginative in a

situation than usual, are undertaking something new, we are likely to hold our audience. The conclusion that in that case perhaps
we might profit by extending our interests,
undertaking new adventures, or bringing
more imagination to our everyday lives can
hardly be escaped. We soon learn to discard a
report of our latest attack of illness, the most
recent exploit of our offspring, the remarkable
intelligence of our pets, today's example of
our bad luck, as opening gambits in adult
conversation. If you are with someone who is
still a slave to that kind of word-wasting, consciously introduce a subject of more depth or
wider interest when it is your turn to speak.
If you discover that he or she stubbornly re-
sists all such invitations to better talk, you
have a decision to make.

There may be, in spite of all limitations,
such warmth, sweetness, genuine feeling in
even a limited friend that one can under no
circumstances think of abandoning the relationship. On the other hand, we sometimes
discover, to our surprised dismay, that we

have attached someone to ourselves for no better reason than that in his presence we can babble on about the trivialities of our lives, though there is no deep bond between us. To withdraw from that association as soon as is consistent with not hurting the other party, to refuse to continue to waste your own energy and time, or connive in the wasting of his, is a plain obligation. If you have been guilty (as most of us have) of forming such an association-in-weakness, the first effort at correction should be to see whether you cannot transform it into a genuine friendship, stimulating and strengthening; only when you must give up all hope of that should the relationship be dropped.

9.

The correction of the "I-mean," the "As-a-matter-of-fact" habit, takes coöperation. If you realize that you have picked up a verbal mannerism, call on the friend to whom you talk most fluently and emotionally. It is fairly easy to control such a mannerism in the pres-

Correct any verbal mannerism
you may have.

ence of someone we hardly know, but in the heat of discourse the offending phrase will crop up in every other sentence. Tell the friend that you are saying "and so on," for instance, to the point of absurdity. Ask him to watch for it, and to hold up his hand without interrupting the conversation whenever he hears you use it. The talk which follows will be choppy, and there is likely for a while to be more laughter than conversation, but you will begin to get the habit in hand. Two or three sessions will entirely eradicate the phrase—except when you actually want to use it.

10.

Plan two hours of a day and live according to the plan.

If you are working by yourself as a free lance, any day will do. If not, choose a Sunday or holiday to experiment on. Make the schedule partly according to your usual habit, partly unlike it. As for instance:

7:30–8 Breakfast and newspaper
8–8:20 Mail

8:20–9:25 Arrange books according to subject matter

9:25–9:30 Telephone (if on weekday) for
some appointment you have
been putting off. If Sunday or
holiday, go out for a walk.

The complexity or diversity of the items has
very little to do with this practice. The point
is to turn from one activity to the next, not at
the *approximate* minute of your schedule, but
on the exact moment. If you are only half-way
through the newspaper, that's very sad. But
down it must go, and you open your mail—
hitherto disregarded. If this is a day without
an incoming mail, the twenty minutes go to
letter-writing. If you have time to spare, send
a card or two, or make notes for another letter
on another day. Wherever you are at 8:20 with
your correspondence, you stop and turn to the
arranging of books. One of your planned activities, at least, should promise a fair amount
of interest to you. If it is not arranging books,
then clipping articles from a magazine can

replace it, or even straightening a room thoroughly.

The twin purposes of this discipline are, first, to give ourselves the experience of being under orders again, and, second, to demonstrate how badly we lose our sense of the time necessary to accomplish any stipulated activity. Every printer that ever lived, probably, has grumbled at an editor or make-up man who wants to crowd too many letters on a line, complaining that "he must think we've got rubber type." Well, most of us think our days have rubber hours. Even those suburbanites who have learned by long experience that it is just seventeen minutes to a second from the shower-bath to the railroad station will nonchalantly plan to cram the work of half a day into a couple of hours after lunch. We expect time to be infinitely accommodating, we refuse to admit that it cannot be. But it is possible to learn—by planning, first, two hours of a day, then three, then four, and so on till we have planned and lived an effective, eight-hour day (at the least)—to use time to the best advantage. Rigid scheduling of a whole day is not always possible or even desirable, but a few days lived by time-table now and again will refresh our sense of the value of time and teach us what we can expect of ourselves when we do not waste it.

For those who need really stern warning about this: one psychiatrist, Dr. Paul Bousfeld, holds that the sure sign of the incurable egotist is that he never allows for the actual amount of time any given activity will take. Firmly, though unconsciously, believing that the world revolves around him, certain of his magical power to arrest the progress of the sun and the moon, he goes through life astonished at the refractoriness of Time in not meeting him half-way. He is always late to appointments, behind in his obligations, constantly assuming more work or accepting more invitations than he could keep if he were twins. He either learns the error of his ways or comes to a bad end.

11.

This is the most difficult of all. It will seem so arbitrary to many readers that they will not even try to apply it. It *is* arbitrary; that is its very essence. It is less necessary for those living in the midst of large families than for persons living alone, or those who are alone most of the time. Remembering the quotation given above from Dr. Carrel, arrange to put yourself into situations where you *must* act non-habitually, where you must adapt yourself. Members of the Army, the Navy, the priesthood, some societies, are constantly in a state of living under orders; and we recognize in them a resiliency that is absent from the characters of most men and women who live according to their own convenience. It is not easy to get this resiliency back into our lives, but it is a quality too valuable to be lost. If the following recommendation seems somewhat too dramatic, almost too ridiculous, be assured that the results will show the worth of the discipline.

On a number of slips of paper—twelve will do to start with—write instructions like these:

"Go twenty miles from home, using ordinary conveyance." (In other words, don't just get out a car or hire a taxi, if you can afford it, and drive somewhere. Take street-cars, buses, ferries, subways.)

"Go twelve hours without food."

"Go eat a meal in the unlikeliest place you can find." A restaurant in a totally foreign quarter of a city is good here. Asking for food at a farm-house is better, if you are hardy enough to be so unconventional.

"Say nothing all day except in answer to questions."

"Stay up all night and work."

And this, by the way, is the most valuable order of them all. You must plan to work steadily and quietly, resisting every temptation to lie down for a few moments, but relaxing very slightly against the chair-back every hour or so, bracing yourself to your work again the moment lassitude threatens to overcome you. Only those who have actually done this realize that there are depths to our minds which we seldom plumb, accustomed as we are to succumb to the first attack of fatigue, or staying awake only so long as we have outer stimulation.

Seal these slips of paper in twelve envelopes, shuffle them thoroughly and put them in a drawer. Whenever you think of it, shuffle them again. Every other week, or on a given day of each month, pick one of the envelopes, open it, and perform your own command. It may be raining pitchforks on the day you command yourself to travel twenty miles by common carrier; nevertheless, unless your state of health absolutely forbids it, you go. If you are doing an intensive piece of work, one monthly exercise of this sort is enough. If not, the oftener you can be arbitrary with yourself—without turning into a restless jumping-jack, it goes without saying—the better for your character eventually.

There need not be twelve different orders on your slips. If you can think of activities which are genuinely difficult for you to do,

which go against the grain but which you yet
know would be valuable training for you, include them. One young man of my acquaintance who was abnormally shy insisted to himself that he should get into conversation with
at least three strangers daily. Any activity you
choose should be both corrective and unusual,
cutting abruptly across your usual routine.

12.

An alternative method is this: from time to
time give yourself a day on which you say
"Yes" to every request made of you which is
at all reasonable. The more you tend to retire
from society in your leisure, the more valuable this will be. You may find yourself invited to go sleigh-riding in your twenty-four
hours; you may be invited to change your job.
The sleigh-ride should certainly be accepted,
however much you may hate straw, thick
blankets and cold weather. The job-changing,
fortunately, can be submitted to examination,
since it is only "reasonable" activities which
you are to undertake without second thought.
Don't be afraid nothing will occur on that

day; it is astonishing how many small requests
we can turn aside daily rather than interrupt
our even course. The consequences may be
wide-reaching, often educative, sometimes extremely advantageous.* Nevertheless do not
jump to the conclusion that because one day
of the sort has brought so many interesting

* The first time I put this discipline into practice,
for example, I was asked, for the first time in years,
to teach a class in fiction-writing. Now I had
always said on every occasion that I abhorred
teaching, that I would never teach while I had the
sense to make a living any other way, that most of
the courses in fiction-writing I had seen did almost
nothing for the pupils. Under my own orders, I
had to accept: I was qualified by having written
fiction myself, by ten years of editing, by having a
few ideas for starting the flow of writing. I took
the class, listened to the questions my students
asked me, discovered that no book I knew of
answered them fully—and was led into writing one
of my own. . . . And this present book is the result
of another such "Yea-saying" day. The lecture I
was asked to give came at a time when my schedule
was more than full, when I would, if I had not
given myself blanket instructions to accept, have
begged off on that occasion. Not every day of the
sort has quite such far-reaching consequences, but
in my life they are almost always interesting, if
nothing more.

possibilities to light, *every* day should be led in that manner. On the contrary; to deny one-self an opportunity now and again is fully as illuminating, particularly for those who waste too much time in party-going, theatres, and so on. Such persons should plan to refuse many invitations, and spend the time in intensive self-cultivation.

On this system, work out other disciplines which are good for your individual case. There are two ways of making them. First, become aware of some weakness or inadequate performance on your part; then decide, perhaps after experiment, whether the way to correct it is to set yourself to doing the exact opposite, or whether—as in curing the habit of talking too much about one's own interests —acting a ludicrous and over-emphasized parody of the failing will be more effective.

Once you get the idea, you will find these disciplines not only helpful but genuinely amusing. In many cases they replace the rather haphazard puzzle-solving activities which call on somewhat the same capacities. In matching your wits against yourself you take on the shrewdest and wiliest antagonist you can have, and consequently a victorious outcome in this duel of wits brings a great feeling of triumph. At last, when one is in training, one can call at will on any of the mental traits which have been strengthened or exercised in these ways and find that it performs exactly and quickly.

But, as you begin to take pleasure in these exercises, remind yourself that *they are means, not ends.* In getting control of your mind you are not yet using it officially, so to speak. You are still in your probationary period. Have you ever met one of those health-seekers who eat just so many ounces of food per day, walk just so many miles or play just so many games of handball, sit in the sun or under a sun-lamp just so many minutes—and then lead the dullest of personal lives? He has made himself into a magnificently healthy creature —for no purpose whatsoever. You are training your mind in order to engage it in definite activity, so do not put off too long the matter of getting at your original plans.

III

Still considering what aids we can find to successful living, but now in the way of direct support for ourselves, there are various ways in which we can make the process smoother. One of the best is to follow the suggestion of Franklin, in his *Autobiography,* and to check daily on our progress by means of a small, specially prepared notebook. Franklin himself drew up a list of thirteen Virtues, and under each wrote a maxim embodying the sense of that virtue to his mind. For instance, under Temperance he wrote "Eat not to dullness; drink not to elevation"; under Silence: "Speak not but what may benefit others or yourself; avoid trifling conversation"; and so went on, through Order, Resolution, Frugality and the rest. It is hardly possible to draw up a better set, but—and perhaps it is one more sign of the softening of the race—for most purposes the six matters which we find most troublesome will seem quite enough for our present purposes.* Each will have his own set of faults to be corrected. But let us say, for instance, that you decide you could do more work if you would; that you are shy; that you take too long to make up your mind; that you talk too much (and timidity and talkativeness are by no means mutually exclusive vices); that you eat at odd hours or the wrong things; that you sleep too long (or not enough). Your notebook-page should look like this:

	S	M	T	W	T	F	S
WORK	√						
COURAGE							
DECISION	√ √						
SPEECH	√ √						
MEALS	√						
SLEEP							

The checks represent your estimate of the number of times you successfully resisted the

* Any reader who can do so should look into the *Autobiography;* it is full of excellent suggestions.

temptation to act in the unsatisfactory way. As you find yourself able to fill any of the squares of your notebook each day—in other words, when you have eradicated the trouble-making fault—you can retire that classification and replace it with another which you may have noticed. If you soon outgrow the need of the notebook, splendid. It can be kept in a convenient drawer, though, as a reminder.

Then there is the matter of getting into the day. Those who wake fully each morning would find it hard to believe how many of their fellows suffer from not being fully in command of their faculties in the morning. If you belong to the latter crew, don't hesitate to imitate the Katherine Mansfield hero who woke, opened his eyes, and saw the sign he had put up for himself: "Get out of bed at once."

What is more, if you *know*—as so many of us do—that at midnight you have a genuine inspiration which your morning's prosaic mood leads you to disregard, write yourself a note about it. Be pretty firm about the matter; put it sharply. Say to yourself, in writing, "You're an idiot if you don't at least see whether Macy's would like that idea. Make an appointment today!" Often nothing more is needed to make the prosy, unimaginative daylight mood break up and allow the intenser one to return.

One of the most famous men in America constantly sends himself post-cards, and occasionally notes. He explained the card-sending as being his way of relieving his memory of unnecessary details. In his pocket he carries a few postals addressed to his office. I was with him one threatening day when he looked out the restaurant window, drew a card from his pocket and wrote on it. Then he threw it across the table to me with a grin. It was addressed to himself at his office, and said "Put your rain-coat with your hat." At the office he had other cards addressed to himself at home.

Rewarding oneself for successful work—even in addition to the success—is another way of promoting proper action. If you get yourself some small luxury when, and only when, your notebook shows a week of satisfactory marks, you may go to slightly more trouble to turn away from your faults.

Get into the habit of being both strict and friendly toward yourself: demand a certain standard of performance; approve of yourself, even reward yourself, if you attain it. Far too often we pursue just the wrong tactics. When we should be acting we indulge or excuse ourselves for inactivity; we then upbraid and punish ourselves ruthlessly and futilely. The scolding is futile because we somehow feel that, if we have been severe and cutting to ourselves, we have in some way atoned for the fault of non-performance. We have not, of course. We have not done what we planned, and we have discouraged and hurt ourselves into the bargain.

CHAPTER XII

—AND THE BEST OF LUCK!

S UMMING up, then, we have as the first tenet of success: Act as if it were impossible to fail.

Beginning to put this into practice, we discover that the first demand upon us is that we should reclaim as much as possible of the energy which now goes into revery or into time-killing, and devote it to purposeful activity, to action-toward-an-end. We act by ignoring all memories or apprehensions of failure, by refusing to attach importance to temporary discomfort or past pain. We learn not to court frustration by using an attitude or tone which leaves any opportunity for rebuff or non-coöperation. We exercise our minds in trial-performances in order to have them fully under our control when the occasion to use them in an expert way arises. With the imagination we painlessly explore all the possible reaches of our lives and constantly provide ourselves with prospects of future interests to such an extent that we shall not fall back into day-dreaming.

We deliberately make for ourselves an invigorating mental climate, and in this atmosphere, freed of doubts and anxieties, we act.

In the last few chapters we have been considering these facets of successful action one by one. Now it must be remembered that, however correct and suggestive such detailed considerations may be, they suffer badly in one manner: their tempo, so to speak, has had to be altered in order to show them minutely.

A slow-motion picture of ball-players in action, of golfers, of a tennis-match, is sometimes of inestimable value to those who are learning to play. The muscular effort behind a sudden dextrous turn of the body, in its normal tempo far too quick for the eye to catch, is shown in the retarded film in all its subtlety. But we gain our insight into the technique of difficult plays by losing sight, for the moment, of another aspect. You will remember how, in such pictures, the player glides languorously through the air, the ball curves slowly towards the racquet, touches it with a soft impact and slides slowly away again. Illuminating as these pictures are, they are also always irresistibly comic: the leap, the crack, the rapidity of the game as we know it is gone, replaced by a twilit, dreaming gentleness.

Now, to consider the technique of success in these pages, we have had to sacrifice pace to analysis in just this way. The actual tempo of success, while it should not have the nervousness or strain that is almost inevitable in a competitive contest, is quicker, smoother, more brisk than any book analyzing it can ever show. There is a delightful conciseness in successful action. "I know I'm doing a good picture if I'm painting just as fast as I can move," a great artist said to a group of friends recently. "The minute I dabble I know I'm stalling, that there's something I'm not seeing right; when I'm right its almost like play."

There is undoubtedly something game-like about pertinent activity: those distressful clichés of a few years ago, "the advertising game," "the engineering game," "the restaurant game," had some excuse in reality. The vocabulary of men who are successful in the sense that they have amassed huge fortunes abounds in terms taken over from the jargon of sports: "A fast one," "Out of bounds," and so on. And however unlike the big-business ambition of such a man one's own personal idea of success may be, there is something to be deduced from the frequency of recreation-terms when stories of success are in question. Purposeful action seems quicker, clearer, more straightforward and enjoyable than any other. In reality, you may be working more slowly and carefully than ordinarily; still, the fact that there is no confusion of issues, no part of your mind off wool-gathering as you move, gives an unmistakable "tone" to activities which are being carried on in the proper way.

It is just this tone that you are setting yourself to recapture by imagination when you remember the mood of an earlier success. Once you have found it in the past, made use of it for present action, and noted the similarity in pace which results, you will soon be able to strike the right rhythm without the elaborate preliminary imaginative activity. Further, this rhythm sometimes crops out unexpectedly, in the middle of unimportant events; it is a promise that, if you can get away and at work, you will find yourself "in vein." So you will come to recognize its onset and be able to turn it to your advantage.

This feeling of pace, or tone, or rhythm— it represents itself differently to differing temperaments—will be your evidence that you are headed the right way. This is no recommendation to hasten your physical action in working. That may or may not come to pass. Very often it does; in other cases undue haste

has been one of the contributions of the Will
to Fail, which, aping the decisiveness of au-
thoritative motion, allowed several essentials
to good work to be overlooked or skimped.

It is not so much any real briskness that is
being considered here as it is the fact that un-
impeded movement in a forward direction is
pleasant and rhythmical, movement which
goes unwaveringly towards success.

Let us, for another *reductio ad absurdum*,
consider one great class of successes, of which
almost everyone has had some personal experience, or at the very least has met in the
lives of those about him: the state called the
courage of desperation.

In the most extreme cases, this courage
arises because some catastrophe or series of
misfortunes has *completely wiped out every
alternative to success*. "He has nothing to
lose," we say of one in this situation. Very well,
then; he acts with a directness and daring
which he could not ordinarily command. So
often that it has become a matter of legend for
us, this action is attended with overwhelming

success. If you will remember the third victim of the Will to Fail in an earlier chapter, you will recall that he had made a state of desperation into a superstitious prerequisite to accomplishment. Quite misreading the situation, he came to believe that the prospect of utter vanquishment would, each time, cause Fate to relent. What he entirely overlooked was that when he had reached such straits that he *dared not* fail he invariably acted as he should always act: as if it were impossible to fail. Without exception in this state he succeeded. Inextricably involved in the meshes of his bad and emotional thinking, he invited failure as the only way to spur himself to effort. To his acquaintances he inevitably recalled the crazy hero of world-wide fame, the man who hit himself on the head with a hammer because it felt so good when he stopped. It was and is all very serious to him.

But remove the absurdity from these examples of the courage of desperation, and we have the sense. Desperation does cut off one alternative. But desperation is not needed, is not the only tool which will cut away the possibility of failure. Imagination will do the work even better and more neatly. And we are left with Courage-facing-in-the-right-direction.

Courage facing in the right direction is the *sine qua non* of success. It is to reach that stage that we put ourselves through exercises in flexibility and restraint, learn to turn imagination away from apprehension and into useful channels, determine to act wisely in minor matters in order to store up courage for the major issues of our lives. We use our heads to get the greatest good from our gifts and abilities, refusing ourselves the weakening privileges of dreaming, avoiding responsibilities, following the line of least resistance, acting childishly.

Success, for any sane adult, is exactly equivalent to doing his best. What that best may be, what its farthest reaches may include, we can discover only by freeing ourselves completely from the Will to Fail.

THE END

A Personal Word from the Author

ANY book which has been found helpful is likely to be read more than once. If, sooner or later, you re-read this one, you might take that opportunity to make it still more useful to you every time you turn back to it. Perhaps some passages clarified an idea in your mind, or resolved some doubt. Perhaps you found other things which you felt you already knew but tend, somehow, to forget. Here and there you may find a sentence that might have been written with your case directly in mind.

Don't let respect for the printed page keep you from turning just *a* book into *your* book. Read with a pencil in hand. When you come to a passage you believe you may consult often, or may need to re-fresh your memory upon later, draw a long line down the margin of the page. Sentences or para-graphs which are personally useful to you should be underlined. Then, in the back of the book, write down the numbers of the pages on which such markings occur, with perhaps a word or two as clue to what may be found there. You can cross out with a large X any page with which you disagree, or strike out any sentence not applicable to your life. If you have a comment or extension of your own to make, write it into the margin.

All handbooks are much more satisfactory when privately edited in this way. The more personally serviceable they are the nearer they come to fulfill-ing their author's intention. Make what you need stand out at a glance; save yourself waste motion by eliminating superfluous pages. In this way you can collaborate with any handbook's author in doing what he most hopes to do: to make a book which is personal, practical, helpful, for every individual reader.

About the Author

DOROTHEA BRANDE was born in Chicago in 1893.
After attending the University of Chicago and
the University of Michigan she held editorial
and reportorial jobs on the *Journal of the American
Medical Association,* the *Chicago Record-
Herald,* and the *Chicago Tribune.* She spent
three years as circulation manager of the *American
Mercury* when it was under the editorship
of H. L. Mencken and then became associate
editor of the *Bookman* under Seward Collins.
When Mr. Collins replaced the *Bookman* with
the *American Review,* Mrs. Brande continued
with the new magazine but presently began
writing books, delivering lectures, and conduct-
ing courses in short story writing. In 1934 her
first book, *Becoming a Writer,* made its appearance. It was followed in 1935 by *Most Beautiful
Lady,* a detective story that was published in
England under the title, *Beauty Vanishes.* Reading philosophy comes first among Mrs. Brande's
hobbies, travel by sea comes second, and watching cats—of which she has five—comes third. Her
book and courses on writing have brought her a
growing correspondence from all parts of the
nation.